CONCILIUM

Religion in the Seventies

CONCILIUM
Religion in the Seventies

EDITORIAL DIRECTORS: Edward Schillebeeckx (Dogma) ·
Herman Schmidt (Liturgy) · Alois Müller (Pastoral) ·
Hans Küng (Ecumenism) · Franz Böckle (Moral Theology) ·
Johannes B. Metz (Church and World) · Roger Aubert (Church
History) · Teodoro Jiménez Urresti (Canon Law) · Christian
Duquoc (Spirituality) · Pierre Benoît and Roland Murphy
(Scripture)

CONSULTING EDITORS: Marie-Dominique Chenu · ✠Carlo
Colombo · Yves Congar · Andrew Greeley · Jorge Mejía ·
Karl Rahner · Roberto Tucci

EXECUTIVE SECRETARY: (Awaiting new appointment),
Arksteestraat 3–5, Nijmegen, The Netherlands

Volume 64: Ecumenism

EDITORIAL BOARD: Walter Kasper · Gregory Baum ·
René Beaupère · Carlos de Céspedes · Robert Clément ·
Jean Corbon · Avery Dulles · Herman Fiolet · Alexandre
Ganoczy · Manuel Gesteira Garza · Jan Groot · Gotthold
Hasenhüttl · Michael Hurley · Antonio Javierre · Bernard
Lambert · Emmanuel Lanne · Hervé Legrand · Marie-Joseph
Le Guillou · Peter Lengsfeld · Joseph Lescrauwaet ·
Hendrik van der Linde · Antonio Matabosch · Jorge Mejía ·
Harry McSorley · John Oesterreicher · Daniel O'Hanlon ·
Otto Pesch · Olivier Rousseau · Alfonso Skowronek · Georges
Tavard · Gustave Thils · Maurice Villian · Edward Vogt ·
Wilhem de Vries · Jan Witte

PAPAL MINISTRY
IN THE CHURCH

Edited by

Hans Kung

Herder and Herder

1971
HERDER AND HERDER NEW YORK
232 Madison Avenue, New York 10016

CONTENTS

Editorial   7

PART I

ARTICLES

Questions for the Papacy Today   12
CHARLES DAVIS

The Position and Significance of Peter in the Church
of the New Testament   21
RUDOLF PESCH

Roman Primacy in the First Three Centuries   36
JAMES F. McCUE

THEORETICAL AND PRACTICAL RENEWALS
OF THE PRIMACY OF ROME

1. The Development after Constantine   45
   WILHELM DE VRIES

2. From the Early Middle Ages until the Gregorian
   Reform   54
   HORST FUHRMANN

THE PAPACY AND THE REFORMATION

1. To what Extent is Roman Primacy unacceptable to
   the Eastern Churches?   62
   EMMANUEL LANNE

2. Would the Pope still have been the Antichrist for
   Luther today?   68
   WENZEL LOHFF

Why was the Primacy of the Pope defined in 1870?   75
VICTOR CONZEMIUS

How can one evaluate Collegiality vis-à-vis Papal
Primacy?   84
ALEXANDRE GANOCZY

ADVANTAGES AND DRAWBACKS OF A
CENTRE OF COMMUNICATIONS IN THE
CHURCH

1. Historical Point of View   95
   JOHN E. LYNCH

2. Sociological Point of View   101
   ANDREW M. GREELEY

CAN A PETRINE OFFICE BE MEANINGFUL
IN THE CHURCH?

1. A Greek Orthodox Reply   115
   STYLIANOS HARKIANAKIS

2. A Russian Orthodox Reply   122
   PAUL EVDOKIMOV

3. An Anglican Reply   127
   ARTHUR M. ALLCHIN

4. A Protestant Reply   132
   HEINRICH OTT

5. An Attempt at a Catholic Answer   139
   HERMANN HÄRING

PART II

BULLETIN

The Results of Recent Historical Research on
Conciliarism   148
PAUL DE VOOGHT

In memoriam: Paul Evdokimov   158
ALEXANDRE GANOCZY

Editorial

WHAT is the greatest difficulty on the way to ecumenical agreement between the Christian Churches? The problems centre upon the understanding of what the Church really is. But in regard to the general understanding of the Church as the community of the faithful, as the people of God, the body of Christ, a spiritual entity; in regard to the characteristics of the Church, and, indeed, to some principles of ecclesiastical organization: in these respects, nowadays, the number of necessarily divisive differences between the Churches is constantly dwindling. As the 1968 Ecumenism number of this journal showed, it is even possible to discuss reasonably and sympathetically the question of the apostolic succession.

In its consideration of "post-ecumenical Christianity" the 1970 Ecumenism number gave an unequivocal answer to my question: the Papacy is the greatest difficulty! It cannot be affirmed too emphatically that the paradox of all paradoxes is to be found in the fact that the very ecclesiastical institution that claims to be the rock of unity has made itself *the* monolithic obstacle to the unity of the Church: for the Catholic Church and the Protestant Churches, for the Western as for the Eastern Church, for Anglicans just as much as for Old Catholics.

Can this obstacle be removed? There are always those who are deceived into thinking that ecumenical understanding can be achieved despite institutions. This is certainly true in the case of small groups, but not for the Churches. In order to reach the large-scale and enduring goal, a sort of "long march" by way of the institutional Churches is unavoidable. Of course there are also victims of illusion within the Catholic Church, who now affirm that ecumenical agreement can be realized without reference to the Papacy. To be sure, in parishes and in some countries much can and ought to be done in the way of ecumenism, without Rome, or in by-passing Rome, or even in contradiction to Rome. The ultimate standard for the ecumenical movement can never be the Roman *Codex Iuris Canonici* or the will of the Pope, but ever and only the will of God as expressed in the gospel of Jesus Christ. But even for the Catholic Church, on the whole and in the long run, a truly ecumenical goal can be attained only if the problem of the Papacy is *not* circumvented. Much in the Church and in Christianity can and must be managed pragmatically and not dogmatically. But an ecumenical agreement reached without reference to the quest for truth can only superficially patch up and not heal the wounds.

There are two related though distinct aspects to the problem of the Papacy seen from an ecumenical perspective, which were clearly distinguished even by Vatican I: papal primacy and papal infallibility. When the newly awakened discussion in the Catholic Church about the question of infallibility can be viewed more precisely, we hope to treat the problem of the Pope's infallibility in a special issue of *Concilium*. The theme of this issue is the papal primacy, which in any case provides the basis for the papal claim to infallibility.

As Editor, I thought it was important to allow the first word to the theologian and friend who supported the Papacy throughout a long career as a theologian, and who finally surrendered ecclesiastical office in the Catholic Church on account of the Papacy: Charles Davis has formulated the problem, as he sees it today, nicely and objectively. I hope that the entire number will show him how far the difficulties are realized today in the Catholic Church as well.

In order to answer the questions posed here we have assembled a collection of commentators with very different viewpoints. The end-effect, however, is not cacophony, but an emphasis on certain common themes and tendencies. Both R. Pesch's report on the exegetical standpoint, and the historical analyses of McCue, de Vries, Fuhrmann, de Vooght and Conzemius show

how very necessary it is to distinguish between a Petrine office
that can possibly be justified on a New Testament basis, and the
Papacy as it has developed, grown—and even grown awry.
Lanne's and Lohff's comments on the Papacy and the division
of the Church lend weight to this viewpoint.

Obviously this issue would be incomplete were it restricted to
exegetical and historical critiques. As a Catholic journal, *Concilium* must stress the positive significance of a centre of communication in the Church; Ganoczy, Lynch and Greeley have
set themselves this task. The other Churches were set the question of whether a Petrine office could have any meaning in the
Church: St. Harkianakis, Evdokimov, Allchin and Ott offer their
several answers. In his turn, H. Häring has tried to provide a
Catholic reply to these answers—a reply with which I, as Editor
of this issue, entirely agree.

Our intention is not to convert anyone to advocacy of a Petrine
office in the Church, let alone to turn anyone against it, but
honestly and precisely to provide material for consideration—
and for action. This at least ought to become clear upon a reading of this issue: If a Petrine office is still to have any meaning
today in the Catholic Church and in Christendom, then that
meaning depends upon a renunciation of certain legal prerogatives and positions of spiritual power that that have accrued to
it in the course of history. As the present issue very clearly
demonstrates, the Papacy as it is today depends in many respects
not upon the original commission, but upon a very problematical
historical development. A radical reordering of that office in the
light of the Christian Gospel seems inevitable. This is possible
and, indeed, is in some small measure already on the way to
accomplishment. In this regard, with certain indisputable limitations, John XXIII indicated the way to a conception of the possible Pope of the future. Ultimately, however, it is not a matter
of the Pope. For a Christian—and hence for the Pope himself as
well—it is a matter of Jesus Christ alone!

Two things must be done immediately:

1. *The Pope must be elected by an authoritative body that is
truly representative of the Church.* The exclusion of cardinals
who are older than eighty is a courageous step on the part of

Pope Paul VI, but only a first step. The present College of Cardinals represents neither the different nations nor the various mentalities nor the various age-groups within the Church.

2. *There must be an age-limit for the Pope too.* The age-limit of seventy-five for bishops is quite excessive in comparison to other positions of responsibility in public life. The incomparably more important task of the Pope demands an age-limit that is just as fixed, and preferably even lower. Exceptions confirm the rule: the Church would not have been harmed had John XXIII become Pope a few years before he did assume office. A Pope with a recognized time-limit, and therefore a more exact distinction between office and individual, would make the character of the Petrine office as an office of service much clearer.

HANS KÜNG

PART I
ARTICLES

Charles Davis

Questions for the Papacy Today

I. Two Worlds

QUESTIONS are now crowding upon the papacy from every side. To interpret the present situation with its complex pressures we must try to discern some underlying pattern. Is there a fundamental issue behind the different demands, hopes, questions and appeals directed at the papacy today? I suggest that we can make sense of present stresses in this way: a papacy culturally estranged from the modern world is now being strongly pressed to become catholic, in the sense of once more in harmony with the existing range of human and Christian resources.

So, the papacy is in trouble because not actually catholic, having failed to keep up with human developments it should have assimilated. To say this does not necessarily imply a rejection of the papacy. Many Catholics are saying the same. They add that the papacy remains potentially catholic and hence reformable. But I have no wish to dispute that here. In what everyone regards as a difficult transitional period I want to help if I can by examining the reasons for the obstinately persistent clash of the papacy with the modern world.

Briefly, then, it is a question of two worlds. The world of the papacy, the world to which it was related for centuries and which to some extent it created, has through various cultural changes ceased to be the world of Western men. With the rapid disappearance of a cultural lag this is now true of Catholics themselves. The papal world was never more than potentially catholic in relation to mankind as a whole; culturally the papal world was limited to the West. Now, however, the horizon of the papal world is too narrow to include the world of modern Western men, let alone the even wider world of a unified mankind now sensed to be just beyond our present horizon. The papacy is struggling to overcome the myopia caused by the fixation of its focus within the limits of its traditional world, but it has not yet succeeded in doing so. Certainly, no one is asking for an uncritical acceptance of everything modern, but the concern is with genuine developments in human consciousness and life since the papacy took shape and marked out its world.

Now, the papacy cannot enter the world in which men now live while itself remaining unchanged. The relation between a person and his world, between an institution and its world, is always bilateral. To be in a world is not just a question of taking cognizance of it; it presupposes a process from which both sides, person or institution and world, emerge mutually transformed and thus mutually related. Papal authority cannot thrust itself unchanged into the world of modern men.

Its attempts to do just that are failing. Authority, the philosophers tell us, as distinct from mere power includes acceptance in its very concept. It is contradictory to speak of authority where there is no recognition of it. Even the authority of God connotes the acceptance it evokes. On this understanding there has undoubtedly been a rapid diminution of papal authority among Catholics during the last few years, namely since the Church became open to modern culture with the Second Vatican Council but without a corresponding change in the papacy. A general loss of confidence has robbed papal statements and directives of effective force.

To denounce the current attitude to the papacy as a sinful lack of faith and obedience is not particularly helpful. Even devout Catholics find themselves quite unable to give the traditional kind of acknowledgment to papal authority; they would in fact have to cease to belong to the modern world to do so. Nor is the present breakdown of papal authority explained simply by the content of recent decrees. Fundamentally what is at issue is the form and mode of papal authority. Admittedly, those who call for a radical overhaul of the structure of the papacy generally deplore the content of recent papal utterances. All the same, their chief objection is to the obsolete form of the papacy, which they see as inevitably producing such unsatisfactory decrees.

To put it in this way: the present *self-understanding* of the papacy, a self-understanding manifested in its statements and activity and having a long though complex history behind it, is *seriously questioned* by Catholics today, ordinary faithful as well as theologians and ecclesiastics. They are expecting a radical reinterpretation of the nature and role of the papacy. The papacy cannot regain an authority even among Catholics unless it alters its self-understanding and undergoes the transformation necessary to relate it to the world of modern men.

But *why* is the present self-understanding of the papacy out of keeping with modern culture? Why is the papal world not the world of modern men?

The temptation at this point is to delay over more superficial and therefore more easily handled symptoms, such as the methods of the Roman Curia, official secretiveness, slowness in moving towards a collegiate exercise of authority, dubious political and social entanglements. The essential difference with modern culture lies deeper and is harder to formulate. We may look at it from *two angles*: first, the change that has taken place in the understanding of the sacred and its mediation; second, the effects of pluralism.

II. A COSMOCENTRIC VIEW OF THE SACRED

Modern culture is secular. The sacred or transcendent even when not directly rejected has no function in everyday living. Culturally the sacred has become a marginal extra. There is reason, however, to think that this state of affairs is not final and that a reinterpretation of the place of the sacred and the manner of its mediation is in process. The need for a new approach is felt by believers themselves. Their sense of the sacred is troubled and confused at present, because much in traditional religion goes against what they find undeniably true regarding man and the world, reality and values. Hence present discussions about a new formulation of the sacred and about new forms of expression for man's transcendent concern.

What is excluded for men today is a cosmocentric interpretation of the sacred. I mean the view which saw an unchanging cosmic order as the appropriate sign of the presence and action of the sacred. The cosmic order was conceived hierarchically as a great chain of being leading upwards to God at the summit. As divinely given it was regarded as unalterable and independent of man. Its range was not restricted to physical nature: the social order was included in it, so that society and its institutions were likewise seen as permanent, God-given and outside the scope of human creativity. In brief, a cosmocentric view of the sacred prevails wherever an existing order is presented as divinely established not historically achieved and as an immutable norm, so that any tampering with the way things are is regarded as impious.

The world of modern men is historical. Therefore anthropocentric not cosmocentric. The primary feature of reality for men today is not permanence and unchanging order but change and process. In particular, man himself is seen as a self-creative process. He makes both himself and the world in which he lives; or, better, makes himself in his world. Nature is now an evolving process for men to direct and use in their becoming. As for the social order, it is not given by God or cosmic forces, but is the result of human creativity in history and always subject to change through social action.

After the emergence of historical consciousness, it will no longer serve to present the sacred as manifested in an unchanging, hierarchical cosmic order and as mediated through social institutions coming straight from God and thus removed from the creativity and flux of history. Any such view of the sacred can only be regarded today as a surviving remnant of a past mythical view of the world. For an anthropocentric age, the sacred will be disclosed and mediated in and through the human, historical world. In other words, the God whom men will recognize will come not as the architect of some ideal, ahistorical and unchanging order but as the source and sustainer of the free activity of men in making themselves and their world. Modern men will find a sacred or transcendent dimension in so far as they learn to see their self-creativity as rooted in the ultimate reality of God.

The present cosmic order has evolved, and all social institutions, including those of religion, have their history. God does not thrust immutable social and religious institutions upon men, any more than he imposes an unchanging cosmic order upon nature. Hence no claim to possess an authoritative set of sacred institutions coming ready-made from God will carry conviction today. Institutions with sacred authority are not excluded, but provided they make no pretence of bypassing human historical creativity. Institutions are sacred by being the result and expression of men's free relationship with the transcendent, a relationship given and sustained by grace but still human and historical.

The papacy in its present form belongs to the medieval cosmocentric world, for which the sacred was mediated by a permanent hierarchical order, cosmic and social, not subject to human questioning or meddling—a world without historical consciousness. The development of the papacy from the French Revolution to the present century has been a rearguard defence of the medieval order against the advance of modern culture. Having lost touch with the secular West, the papacy is now rapidly losing touch with a Catholic Church open at last to modern culture. Its own entry into the modern world is blocked by a self-understanding still largely reflecting a cosmocentric view of the sacred.

Even now the papacy presents itself thus: as a permanent sacred institution, part of a divinely established hierarchical order of the Church, it is not a creation of men; though in history, it is not a product of historical causes; while undergoing some development and change in history, the main features of its structure as now manifested are unalterable; since its origin and authority are divine, it is out of place for reformers to urge that its form and modes of working no longer correspond to existing social and political institutions. Such remains the official conviction, justifying resistance to anything more than minor changes.

A brief reference to the traditional distinction between the office or function and the individual person may help clarify the difference between a cosmocentric and anthropocentric interpretation of sacred institutions and authority. In the cosmocentric view the distinction becomes a separation which makes official statements, decrees and actions impersonal, ahistorical, absolute, no longer subject to human limitation and corruption. Because of this conception the Church became an impersonal institution, a sacred officialdom, not as such composed of fallible and sinful human persons, a kind of absolute institution existing between God and men. In the anthropocentric or historical view, the distinction between office and person is simply the necessary distinction between a person's public and private activity. The public activity takes place in a social and legal framework and has social and legal consequences outside the determination of the person himself, but his public activity is still his activity, human activity, subject to the laws and conditions of all human activity and therefore open to enhancement by his good qualities and corruption by his failings. The public activity of sacred officials is not untouched by their own limitations as human beings nor does the claim of sacred authority justify ignoring the laws of human intelligence and behaviour as studied by modern psychology and sociology.

Hence nowadays it is inevitable that any papal statement, such as *Humanae Vitae* on birth control, will be carefully assessed even by loyal Catholics in the light of all the known human factors governing its genesis and content. The idea that God through a sacred authority overrides those factors, so that we should ignore them and simply obey, is repugnant to modern consciousness. For men today it implies a primitive, mythical and alienating concept of God and of sacred authority.

III. The Implications of Modern Pluralism

The second feature of modern culture affecting papal authority is pluralism. From a number of causes no single faith or set of ultimate convictions concerning God, man and the world unites Western men today. Modern culture, though possessing some general characteristics, has not, unlike past cultures, a dominant religious tradition. There is no monopoly over ultimate questions, no general symbolic framework for both society and individual human living. On all ultimate questions modern men are confronted with a variety of conflicting authorities; there is no longer one universally recognized authority they can take for granted.

For the modern believer, therefore, unless he lives in a ghetto or remains a moral infant, a personal choice among differing authorities is unavoidable. No fulminations against private judgment can alter that fact of life in modern society. But this further

2—C.

implies that any authority claiming a person's allegiance must render itself credible to him. And since no intelligent and responsible decision can be in the form of a blank cheque, the subsequent actions of the authority will have to be assessed by the believer as confirming, modifying or destroying his acceptance.

So, to put the matter bluntly: in modern, pluralistic society papal authority must render an account of itself to the faithful; it must be prepared to explain and justify its actions and be open to criticism; it cannot expect obedience except in so far as it takes care that its commands and statements, its mode of exercising its authority are credible. To expect otherwise, to seek a blanket, unquestioning obedience is in the modern situation to ask that its followers be irresponsible infants or other-directed drifters.

My contention has been that the present self-understanding of the papacy is out of keeping with the modern world first because it still reflects a medieval, cosmocentric view of sacred institutions and second because it has not yet come to terms with the consequences of modern pluralism for personal faith. The implications of these two fundamental comments could be deployed over a wide range of matters affecting the nature and forms of papal authority. Concrete suggestions may be found in abundance in recent writing. Basically, however, what is at stake is whether the papacy has the potential catholicity to enter the modern world. I have already indicated that this of its nature demands a transformation on the part of the papacy—an unchanged institution cannot enter a new world. Without however genuinely belonging to the modern world, the papacy will not be able to bear witness in it to God and Christ nor will it achieve an effectual role in the problems of development and unification now facing mankind.

IV. Papal Authority the Key Question

Nevertheless, one must sympathize with the present situation of the Pope. To alter the outlook of an ancient institution is immensely difficult. From the Pope himself downward all admit the need and inevitability of change. But the Pope is presented with incompatible assessments of the nature and extent of the changes required. This creates a dilemma. What is to be done practically? Events do not wait until theoretical solutions have been tranquilly agreed upon. Time and again the Pope has to make a decision and choose either refusing a change that some regard as necessary or accepting a change that others consider destructive. Slowness or reluctance to change is no way out of the dilemma, because it represents a decision against all changes that demand speed for effectiveness. And history, I think, would show that as many if not more institutions have been damaged by slowness to accept inevitable change than by over-rapid adaptation to new situations.

Practical decisions often have to be made before full theoretical clarity is reached; indeed, sometimes only a change in practice allows a theoretical solution to emerge. But present bewilderment, though genuine, is made far worse than it need be by the lack of frankness and free discussion in the Church over the key question of papal authority. I call papal authority the key question, not because it is the most important for man's salvation (far from it!), but because without its solution the way is barred, as events keep showing, to the effectual tackling of other, more important problems by the Catholic Church. But there is a timid reluctance to look the question full in the face. Theologians fear the strong official reaction any call for a radical reinterpretation of papal authority would arouse. The present atmosphere is charged with an only too human but false sensitivity, making it almost impossible calmly to question the present self-understanding of the papacy. Even at the Second Vatican Council there was a glossing over by everyone of the major changes in papal authority necessary for any serious acceptance of collegiality. This was a great mistake, and it created the ambiguity hampering development today.

Might I suggest that present tensions are causing a point, obvious once mentioned, to be overlooked? In the very nature of the case the papacy cannot use the present understanding of its authority as a norm to guide and control all reinterpretations of that authority. To do so is in principle to exclude any change not in conformity with its present self-understanding. But sufficient indications have now accumulated of the need for fundamental changes to justify the papacy in refraining from tying its trust in the promise of the Spirit to a particular concept of its own authority. What is now called for is a more general and basic trust in the presence of the Spirit in the Church. Surely, that is how the Church bends without breaking in difficult transitional periods.

The first to welcome an untrammelled discussion of papal authority should be those convinced of the perennial place of the papacy in the Church, because mere insistence upon its present authority without major change is causing an accelerating diminution of the papacy's role in Catholic life. No urgent appeals for loyal obedience will alter that trend, which is a function of modern consciousness. The papacy has once more to demonstrate its catholicity by entering the world to which Christians as modern men now belong.

Rudolf Pesch

The Position and Significance of Peter in the Church of the New Testament
A Survey of Current Research

THE position and significance of Peter in the Church of the New Testament is the subject of converging and diverging views, which plainly cut across confessional boundaries. What makes such convergencies and divergencies possible is the basic decision to eliminate all prejudice by applying historico-critical methods. And what is particularly striking in view of the nature of the subject is a readiness to enter into "ecumenical" discussion of it, a discussion which is still being carried on right down to the present. And yet in spite of all these factors more recent exegesis has continued to be influenced by confessional considerations. Béda Rigaux published a survey of research in this journal four years ago, entitled "Saint Peter in Contemporary Exegesis".[1] Here he actually held that ". . . no one who deals with the subject can be expected to remain absolutely neutral on such a heady issue".[2] The Belgian scholar committed himself to the following

---

[1] *Concilium* (Sept. 1967), pp. 72–86 (American edn., vol. 27).

[2] *Ibid.*, p. 72 a; cf. H. Küng, *Die Kirche* (Ökumenische Forschungen I, 1) (Freiburg-im-Breisgau, 1967), pp. 544–5: "In that case how is to be explained that the same few words and the same brief statements are interpreted in such diametrically opposite senses by scholars who allege that they are working with the same historico-critical methods? There cannot be any doubt: here the whole personality of the theologian concerned plays its part, and this is a factor which is determined by something more than merely the passages involved. The theologian—one more than another—manifestly approaches precisely this question with a quite special preconception, and one which he is able to revise in the light of what he finds in the texts only to a very limited extent. To put the matter in more concrete terms: the position of the theologian with regard to the papacy today does

cautious prediction: "Only time will tell whether common love for truth and common respect for strict rules of objective interpretation will get the better of confessional disputes."[3]

Now in the last few years deeper insights have been won. The application of the "strict rules of objective interpretation" demands a more comprehensive hermeneutic orientation, and it is bound up with the plan to achieve a presentation of the question which is appropriate to the particular theme under examination and in which all relevant aspects are taken into consideration. In the perspective of this comprehensive presentation of the question individual texts, specific historical questions and theological areas of investigation which overlap with the theme under investigation can be discussed and interpreted "in the manner demanded by the nature of the case".[4]

There is one point which today should be counted as recognized and accepted even though it is far from being self-evident. It is that the various possible approaches to the question, the historico-exegetical one, the systematic and critical one, and the approach from the point of view of fundamental or dogmatic theology, should not be confused with one another. And, furthermore, New Testament research must be careful to maintain the relevant distinctions between the illuminations which historical and traditio-historical investigation have to offer on particular aspects of the matter on the one hand, and on the other the theological evaluation, based on this, of the general witness of the New Testament taken as a whole. According to Wolfgang

---

not leave unaffected the interpretation of the relevant exegetical and historical documents. And in view of the many centuries of controversy which have gone to make up the history of interpretation up to the present we must absolutely conclude: it is not very likely that any greater agreement will be arrived at in the interpretation of the texts if we do not first attain a greater measure of agreement with regard to the role of the papacy today. And not the least of the factors on which this greater measure of agreement with regard to the role of the papacy today depends—indeed it may actually be the primary one—is the papacy itself with its constant tendency to interpret itself as something more than the Petrine ministry."

[3] *Ibid.*, p. 597 b.

[4] Very recently W. Trilling has most strikingly drawn attention to this; cf. his article "Ist de katholische Primatslehre schriftgemäss? Exegetische Gedanken zu einer wichtigen Frage", in *Zum Thema: Petrusamt und Papstum* (Stuttgart, 1970), pp. 51–60.

Trilling[5] the observance of such necessary methodological pro-
cedures as applied to specific details would, amongst other things,
lead to the conclusion "that the New Testament witness as such
is hardly capable of yielding an unambiguous answer to the question of whether the New Testament does or does not recognize
any 'succession' to Peter's position, or any 'Petrine office', or
whether (as O. Cullmann believes) it actually excludes any such
office".

What we shall be attempting in the brief survey which follows
is so to sketch in the outlines of the present state of research into
the question of the position and significance of Peter in the
Church of the New Testament that against the background of
an appropriate presentation of the question (I) we shall be in a
position to speak of the specific historical questions involved
(II) and the relevant areas of theological investigation (III) in a
single concise survey.[6]

[5] *Ibid.*, p. 52.
[6] More recent literature (a selection; see also the work by B. Rigaux
cited in n. 1): J. Betz, "Christus-Petra-Petrus", in *Kirche und Überlieferung*,
J. R. Geiselmann zum 70. Geburtstag (Freiburg-im-Breisgau, 1960), pp.
1–21; G. Bornkamm, "Der Auferstandene und der Irdische (Mt. 28: 16–
20)", in *Zeit und Geschichte*, Dankesgabe an R. Bultmann (Tübingen,
1964), pp. 171–91; G. Bornkamm, "Die Binde- und Lösegewalt in der
Kirche des Matthäus", in *Die Zeit Jesu*, Festschrift für H. Schlier (Frei-
burg-im-Breisgau, 1970), pp. 93–107; J. A. Burgess, *A History of the
Exegesis of Mt. 16: 17–19 from 1781–1965* (Diss., Basle, 1965); F. Christ,
"Das Petrusamt im NT", in *Zum Thema: Petrusamt und Papstum* (Stutt-
gart, 1970), pp. 36–50; H. Clavier, "πέτρος καί πέτρα", in *Ntl. Studien für
R. Bultmann* (Berlin, ²1957), pp. 97–109; O. Cullmann, *Peter: Disciple,
Apostle, Martyr* (London, ²1962); O. Cullmann, *T.W.N.T.* VI, pp. 99 ff.;
E. Dinkler, *R.G.G.*, ³V, cols. 247–9; E. Dinkler, "Petrusbekenntnis und
Satanswort", in *Zeit und Geschichte* (cf. supra), pp. 127–53; E. Dinkler,
"Die Petrus-Rom-Frage", in *Theologische Rundschau* N.F. 25 (1959), pp.
189–230, 289–335; N.F. 27 (1961), pp. 33–4; P. Gaechter, *Petrus und seine
Zeit* (Innsbruck, 1958); D. Gewalt, *Petrus. Studien zur Geschichte und
Tradition des frühen Christentums* (Diss. Heidelberg, 1966); C. Ghidelli,
"Bibliografia Biblica Petrina", in *Scuol. Catt.* 96 (1968), pp. 62–110 (1,310
titles!); W. Grundmann, *Das Evangelium nach Matthäus*, T.H.K.N.T. 1
(Berlin, 1968), pp. 392–6; E. Haenchen, "Petrus-Probleme", in *Gott und
Mensch*, Ges. Aufsätze (Tübingen, 1965), pp. 55–67; F. Hahn, "Die Petrus-
verheissung Mt. 16: 18 f.", in *Materialdienst des Konfessionskundlichen
Institus Bensheim* 21 (1970), pp. 8–13; E. Kertelge, "Die Funktion des
'Zwölf' im Markusevangelium. Eine redaktionsgeschichtliche Auslegung,
zugleich ein Beitrag zur Frage nach dem neutestamentlichen Amtsverständnis", in *Tr. Theol. Z.* 78 (1969), pp. 193–200; T. O. Knoch, "Die

I. Plan for an Appropriate Presentation of the Question

On the basis of certain methodological advances which have been achieved (the methods of traditio-historical and "redaction history" research), and of more precise research into the earliest stages of the Church's history, we are in a position to introduce more accurate distinctions in describing the position and significance of Peter in the Church of the New Testament. The traditions concerning Peter are manifold, and we have to establish the place to be assigned to each of these witnesses in terms both of *geography* and *period* within the Church and its stock of traditions before we can explain historically the agreements or discrepancies between them, and evaluate them theologically.

Christian communities and fields of Church activity emerge and exist side by side with one another or following one upon another. And all these have handed on traditions about Peter which treat of him as the disciple of Jesus, apostle, leader of the primitive community in Jerusalem, member of the college set up there and designated as the "pillar", and missionary. Some of them go so far as to glorify Peter and his "office" or his "offices" in a positive and favourable way, while others describe him in negative and critical terms, and others still give an edifying portrayal

Deutung der Primatstelle Mt. 16 im Lichte der neueren Diskussion", in *Bi. Ki.* 23 (1968), pp. 44–6; J. Ludwig, *Die Primatworte Mt. 16, 18. 19 in der altkirchlichen Exegese*, Ntl. Abh. XIX/4 (Münster, 1952); F. Obrist, *Echtheitsfragen und Deutung der Primatstelle Mt. 16, 18 f. in der deutschen protestantischen Theologie der letzten dreissig Jahre* (Münster, 1960); K. H. Schelkle, "Petrus in den Briefen des NT", in *Bi. Ki.* 23 (1968), pp. 46–50; J. Schmid, "Petrus 'der Fels' und die Petrusgestalt der Urgemeinde", in *Begegnung der Christen*, O. Karrer zum 70. Geburtstag (Stuttgart-Frankfurt, 1959), pp. 347–72; W. Schrage, "Ekklesia und Synagoge", in *Z.T.K.* 60 (1963), pp. 178–202; E. Schweizer, *Gemeinde und Gemeindeordnung im NT* (Zürich, 1959); P. Stockmeier, "Das Petrusamt in der frühen Kirche", in *Zum Thema* . . . (cf. above), pp. 61–79; H. Thyen, *Studien zur Sündenvergebung im NT und seinen alttestamentlichen und jüdischen Voraussetzungen*, F.R.L.A.N.T. 96 (Göttingen, 1970), pp. 218 ff.; W. Trilling, "Amt und Amtsverständnis bei Matthäus", in *Mélanges Bibliques en hommage au B. Rigaux* (Gembloux, 1970), pp. 29–44; A. Vögtle, "Messiasbekenntnis und Petrusverheissung. Zur Komposition Mt. 16, 13–23 par.", in *Bibl. Zeitschr.*, N.F. 1 (1957), pp. 252–72; 2 (1958), pp. 85–103; A. Vögtle, *L.T.K.* ²II, 480–2; ²VIII, 334–40; ²X, 551–5, 1443–5; A. Vögtle, "Petrus", in *Die Heiligen in ihrer Zeit*, ed. by P. Manns, Vol. I (Mainz, 1966), pp. 62–8; G. Klein, *Rekonstruktion und Interpretation*, Gesammelte Aufsätze (Munich, 1969), pp. 11–128.

of him and hold him up as an example. They have been formed, expounded, interpreted and reinterpreted with and without connection with one another at various periods in the early history of the Church.

The Galilean communities (the synoptic tradition), Jerusalem and its area of influence (Acts), the Syro-Phoenician Church of Antioch (Acts, Paul), the coastal regions of Asia Minor around Ephesus (Jn.), the area of Greece and Macedonia (1 Cor.) as well as of Rome (1 and 2 Pet.) have all given rise to different traditions about Peter. The emergence of these is to be ascribed to different epochs: the lifetime of Jesus himself and the effects which this had upon the earliest traditions, the initial period of missionary activity in the Church; to these are added traditions designed to support the authority of Peter and worked out by those actually involved with him from the first two decades of the Church, as well as witnesses made up of memories of the apostolic epoch but belonging to the later New Testament period.

The gospels, especially the longer gospels (Mt., Lk. and also Acts), contain Jewish and Gentile Christian traditions from later, earlier and very early periods, and upon these an overall redactional unity has been superimposed. But these gospels already reflect a stage of "integration by the Church as a universal whole" (W. Trilling), and (what is peculiar to this stage) sociological and theological conditions which are conducive to an institutionalization of official positions in the Church. Historical and traditio-historical connections, breaks and gaps, developments and cross-currents, episodes and theological convictions, etc., must be comprehensively evaluated in the conditions appropriate to each in turn, and each must be assessed with regard to its special theological bearing. The fact that the position and significance of Peter differed and was interpreted differently in the different areas and epochs of the New Testament age is indisputable.

II. Specific Historical Questions

(a) The following facts about Peter are not in dispute: that he was Simon who came from Bethsaida (Jn. 1. 44) and was married at Capernaum (Mk. 1. 21a, 29; cf. 1 Cor. 9. 5), that he was a fisherman, the son of one Jona (Mt. 16. 17) or John (Jn. 1. 42:

21. 15–17), and that he belonged to the circle of Jesus' disciples, was a follower of Jesus himself and engaged in missionary service.

A further fact which, despite the later "stylization" of his role in the traditions and redaction of the gospels, is certain, is that he here assumed a leading part as the spokesman and representative of the other disciples (cf. Mk. 1. 29, 36). On the basis of the arguments *pro* and *contra* adduced in the discussion of the "Twelve", it is, in the end, surely more probable that these already constituted a distinct body before, and not merely after Easter. And to the extent that this is true, Simon acted as the "first" of them (thus, strikingly relevant to the present question, in Mt. 10. 2). This is plainly reflected, so far as the beginnings of the Jerusalem community are concerned, in the lists of the Twelve (Mk. 3. 16 ff. par.) (cf. also the vocation traditions!). The historicity of the messianic confession of Caesarea Philippi (Mk. 8. 27 ff. par.) (and in certain cases its meaning also), as well as Simon's denial (Mk. 14. 54, 66 f. par.), remain undisputed. At the same time it remains matter for regret that the tradition history of two elements of tradition which are so important and which have been accorded such a significant place in the Gospel (especially in view of the interpretation in Mt. 16. 13 ff.) should remain unexplained as to their origin.

(b) The *honorific name Kepha* (in its Greek adaptation *Kephas* and translated as *Petros*), which was originally intended as a designation of his position, soon came, from being a sobriquet, to be accepted as the proper name "Peter". But Simon would not already have received this name from Jesus himself. This is shown by the fact that, apart from one exceptional usage due to Lucan redaction (Lk. 22. 34), "Simon" is the form of address consistently placed on Jesus' lips. It is also shown from the shifting position of the story of the conferring of the name in the gospels (even in Mk. 3. 16 the placing of this is redactional!) (cf. Jn. 1. 42).[7] Probably he owes it to his steadfast loyalty to Jesus (Lk. 22. 31 f.) and his call to be the first witness to the resurrection of

---

[7] In the literature on Mt. 16. 18 commentators usually speak simply of the "conferring of a name" as though there were no problems involved. Against this it must be pointed out that Matthew does not record the conferring of the name "Peter" by Jesus at all. On the contrary he has already introduced this sobriquet in his version of the vocation story.

Jesus (Lk. 24. 34: *Simon*; 1 Cor. 15. 5: *Kephas*; notice the way in which the honorific name becomes established in the post-Easter tradition!), that is, this name designates him as the one who provides grounds and assurance for the belief of the Church, who strengthens the brethren (Lk. 22. 32) and who guides (Jn. 21. 15–17), as head of the Twelve who gathers together the eschatological community of Israel for the Messiah Jesus, and as the first "Christian".

(c) Apart from Acts 1. 12, 15, we have Paul's assurance for the fact that up to the apostolic Council Peter, together with the Twelve and later as a member of the college of the three "pillars" (Gal. 2), was vested with the *leadership of the primitive community at Jerusalem and the diaspora which was subject to its authority*. The fact that Peter the *apostle* was also the driving force behind the first mission is attested not only by Acts but also to some extent by the vocation story of Mark 1. 16–18, which is an aetiological "legend" (with an historical nucleus from the period of the pre-Easter mission as found in the "fisher of men" saying in v. 17 par. Mt.), though a different redactional form has been imposed on this in Luke. Simon's (!) position as shepherd of Jesus' flock has early (?) roots in the commission of the risen Lord (Jn. 21. 15–17).

It is no longer possible to establish how this position came to be understood in detail first in the sphere of Jewish Christendom and then, still within this sphere, in view of a Gentile Christendom which was achieving outlines of its own, and finally how it was interpreted by Gentile Christendom itself. We have no information whatever with regard to the position of Peter after his departure from Jerusalem, where James the brother of the Lord relieved him of the leadership of the community (this took place after the apostolic Council yet not simply on the occasion of the brief persecution of Agrippa as recorded in Acts 12. 1–19.

At the apostolic Council (Acts 15; Gal. 2) Peter appears as a leader of the Church which had its focal point at Jerusalem (the collection!) and as such favourably disposed to the Gentile mission of Paul (or the Antiochene Church). The later episode at Antioch, in which Paul, who separates himself (and Barnabas!) from Antioch, is subordinate, reveals Peter unmistakably as influenced by James, the representative of a stricter form of Jewish

Christianity, but in no sense as in a subordinate position under James (see immediately below on Mt. 16. 17–19). The "episode" described from a later and in particular from a Pauline point of view in Galatians 2 was presumably occasioned by the formation of a *mixed* community of Gentile and Jewish Christians, which ran counter to the decisions of the Council of Jerusalem. Probably Peter, who had at first shown himself ready to compromise and revise, subsequently, under pressure from Jerusalem, upholds the strict interpretation of the decisions of the Council (the supremacy of the Christians of Jerusalem over the Jewish Christians of Antioch as well, and thereby over the mixed community as a whole).

(d) A thesis which has repeatedly been put forward in recent times, especially by G. Bornkamm,[8] relates to the *place of origin of Matthew 16. 17–19*. It is suggested that "in spite of the numerous Semitisms so often remarked in this passage its origin can hardly be assigned to the Jerusalem community. It is more probable that these origins are to be sought . . . in a place in which Jewish and Gentile Christians did not encounter one another without considerable tensions", namely in Syria, the home of the gospel in which the tradition of Matthew 16. 17–19 has been preserved, and more specifically in Antioch. This thesis makes it no longer possible to uphold the position laid down by Anton Vögtles[9] in the year 1963: "up to now no illuminating explanation has been given of the theory which alleges that the logion of Matthew 16. 18 f. *had its earliest origins in the primitive Church*. In view of the fact that the confession of Caesarea Philippi can hardly be the locus in history for this logion, it is no longer possible today to base this theory about it on the fact that there is no mention of it in Mark 8. 29 f."

G. Bornkamm adduces sound reasons[10] for the hypothesis that

[8] Cf. above, n. 6, "Die Binde- und Lösegewalt). . .", p. 106.

[9] *L.T.K.* ²VIII, 336. My honoured reader has already given me verbal confirmation of the fact that he too regards G. Bornkamm's hypothesis as the most convincing attempt at a solution at the present time.

[10] Cf. above, n. 6, "Die Binde- und Lösegewalt . . .", p. 104: "In his version as it has come down to us in 16. 18 f. Matthew manifestly presupposes the following: (1) The resurrection of Jesus. The (real) futures οἰκοδομήσω, δώσω clearly point to this, as also does the phrase ὃ ἐὰν δήσῃς in vv. 18 ff., which is to be understood in a corresponding sense. (2) A second point which is also presupposed, however, is the delay of the parousia. The

the formulation and the strength of the tradition of Matthew
16. 18 f. are such as to "presuppose" as its *sitz-im-leben* "the
crucial conflict between Paul and Peter at Antioch, and the departure of Paul from the community which up till then had been
purely Hellenistic in character".[11] The tradition of Matthew 16.
18 f. "manifestly reflects an intrusion of elements from Jewish
Christian tradition into Hellenistic Christianity".

Admittedly there is a further point which we have to accept at
the same time with regard to the teaching authority and disciplinary power ascribed to Simon Peter as the "rock" in Matthew
16. 18 f. for the duration of that epoch of the world's history in
which the Church is not to be overcome by evil. The power
ascribed to Simon Peter here can be understood only as a universal expansion (extending it to Hellenistic Christianity) of the
position which he already held in the Jerusalem community and
over Jewish Christians. How far, as compared with this, Peter
was able in fact to assert this position of his and to extend it to
Antioch and over the Antiochenes must remain an open question.

In any case, on the basis of the hypothesis put forward by
G. Bornkamm (at the time the most plausible), the existence of a
"Cephas" party in Corinth (1 Cor. 1. 12; 3. 22) would also become understandable without having to assume (without any
real basis) that Peter himself spent any time at Corinth. Still more
important, Paul's polemic in his First Epistle to the Corinthians,

---

'Church' referred to in the logion is unmistakably an earthly institution
founded upon the teaching authority vested in Peter and intended to last
as long as the world endures, and one which, moreover, is destined to
overcome the threats offered by the powers of death at the end of time
(16. 20). (3) But it is also important that the term by which this universal
Church is designated in the Greek term ἐκκλησία, and that this is introduced immediately without any more detailed explanation here for the
first and only time in the synoptic tradition. According to the careful researches of W. Schrages it can safely be assumed that this self-designation
of the Church was first arrived at in the sphere of Hellenistic-Jewish Christianity, and derives from its origin in this a theological programme which
is directed against the synagogue and the preaching of the law as practised
in this. It is only on this basis that the meaning of the ekklesia (...μου
τήν ἐκκλησίαν) becomes understandable. It is no longer confined to Israel,
but is world-wide and purely christological in its specification. In terms of
content it is Mt. 21. 33–46; 22. 1–14, and above all Mt. 28. 18–20 which
conform most closely to this meaning."

[11] Cf. above, n. 6, "Der Auferstandene und der Irdische . . .", p. 184, with
n. 57.

which is still most readily understood as contesting the Petrine claims (as formulated in Mt. 16. 18 f.), would be made comprehensible: "for no other foundation can anyone lay than that which is laid which is Jesus Christ" (3. 11; cf. 4. 17, 22 f., also 5. 11 and 10. 4; 15. 5 ff.; Gal. 1. 15).

(e) However true it may be that the origin, original interpretation and initial weight attached to the tradition of Matthew 16. 17–19 can only hypothetically be deduced, it is no less true that (in the current state of Matthaean research!) the *Matthaean interpretation* can be discerned: So far as the Syro-Phoenician Church at the time of Matthew is concerned there was no successor to the position ascribed to Peter or to his "Petrine office". On the contrary, Peter is accounted as a guardian, in the initial stages, of the Matthaean tradition of the dominical sayings (the "Jesus" interpretation of the will of God as set forth in the law) and as the authority who supplies a binding interpretation (with eschatological effects!) to these.

Matthew interprets Matthew 16. 18 f. primarily in the sense of a doctrinal authority attributed to Peter (which can also continue after his death) because "in the time of the Church of Matthew he (Peter) could no longer be regarded as having authority in his own person as disciplinary decisions would demand, but surely as guardian and administrator of the teaching of Jesus for the Church".[12]

Matthew 18. 18 shows that "the 'disciplinary power', i.e. the authority to recognize or to withhold membership of the community" is itself something that is claimed by the community as a whole. Matthew 18. 18 is to be regarded by comparison with Matthew 16. 19 as the *later* tradition: "From this we can only conclude that 18. 18 must be the interpretative application of the Petrine saying to the community as a whole, and, moreover, that it has deliberately been formulated as such. This would imply that the community (of Matthew!) legitimately claims for itself the authority imparted to Peter."[13]

(f) It is extremely instructive to notice that in *later New Testament times* in the Church of Matthew Peter is presented as the

[12] G. Bornkamm," Die Binde- und Lösegewalt . . ." (cf. above), p. 103.
[13] W. Trilling, *Zum Thema: Petrusamt und Papstum* . . . (cf. above), p. 57.

Peter's function set apart from other similar functions (the apostolate of Paul, cf. Gal. 2. 11–14) as though it represented the opposite pole to them, or was it rather one among a whole complex of different "forms" through which the Church was administered? Already in the New Testament itself can we establish a change of form taking place between two distinct levels of tradition belonging to two different periods representing the first and second generations of the Church (cf. Acts 1 and 2 Pet.)? Can we establish any integral continuity in the Petrine function between the three other levels which have been mentioned ("the historical Jesus", the Palestinian-Syrian communities, the later level of the Church as a universal whole), or which developments within these levels or strata are to be discerned?[16]

It is clear that such questions necessarily cut across the boundaries of the Petrine traditions. The questions themselves might be multiplied: which of the ecclesiastical "offices" (ministries) to be found in the New Testament are indispensable, constitutive —and in which precise concrete forms? What is the significance of the interest taken by the Church in its developed and unified stage (as represented by the evangelists and later writers of epistles) in the position of Peter, and under what circumstances did this interest grow up? What is the theological relevance of the fact that as the age of the New Testament progressed a process of institutionalization of the Church developed as a matter of necessity, and indeed as something which, from the sociological point of view, was forced upon it? Further, what consequences can legitimately be drawn from the finding "that there is a close historical and material connection between the *"Ecclesia"* considered as the post-Easter fellowship of the believers and the fellowship of the disciples of the pre-Easter period"?[17]

In examining this question it must be remembered that there is a difference which is constitutive for the very existence of the Church between attachment to the risen Lord, on the one hand,

---

[16] *Ibid.*, p. 55.
[17] F. Hahn, cf. above, n. 6, p. 13; cf. also the points put forward by E. Haag, "Die Himmelfahrt des Elias nach 2 Kg 2:1–15", in *Tr.T.Z.* 78 (1969), pp. 18–32, esp. 29–31.

3—C.

and the Master-disciple relationship which prevailed among the followers of Jesus in the pre-Easter stage, on the other.

What theological significance is to be attributed to the fact that historically speaking specific "offices" can be assigned to specific areas of early Christianity, many of which actually have distinctive theological characteristics of their own (Palestinian, Jewish-Christian, Hellenistic-Jewish-Christian, Gentile-Christian, the Church as a developed and integrated unity)?

How in particular are the "offices" of Peter and Paul, and even the increasing influence of James, to be evaluated against this background?

What part is played by the fact that the central significance of Jerusalem for saving history (something which Paul recognizes!) was progressively lost sight of after the city had been destroyed?

What are the implications of the fact "that the prestige enjoyed throughout the entire Church by the 'apostolic rock' in the transition from the primitive Church to the stage of 'early Catholicism' certainly increased, and yet that no New Testament author has seen this as deriving from an official position with a succession extending into the future of individuals equipped with the same or similar powers"?[18]

On any objective view of the theological (and historical) evidence can we defend the argument which seeks to reduce ecclesiastical offices to two in the following terms: "There are in principle only two official positions which are really universal throughout the Church: the office of the apostle which is prior to the Church, and the office of the Christian which is integral to it."[19] The result of this would be that the ministry of Peter would have to be interpreted as a representative, a truly "Catholic" upholding of this office.

Such "questions on which the discussion should gradually be concentrated if we want to escape from the maze of methodological prior assumptions and prejudices, and from presentations of the question which are often still schematic in the extreme",[20]

---

[18] F. Christ, cf. above, n. 6, p. 49.

[19] Thus W. Marxsen, "Das Nachfolge der Apostel. Methodische Überlegungen zur neutestamentlichen Begründung des kirchlichen Amtes", in Der Exeget als Theologe. Vorträge zum NT (Gütersloh, 1968), pp. 75–90, 87.   [20] W. Trilling, Zum Thema ... (cf. above), p. 55.

could, perhaps, if tackled on an open and comprehensive basis, contribute to the result that "the ministry of Peter, his function as rock and shepherd, should, precisely on a Catholic view, constitute the upholding and strengthening of ecclesiastical unity". It should no longer be "a block of granite that bars the way to any mutual understanding on the part of the Christian Churches, a block that is so great that it seems that we can neither move it nor climb over it nor get round it". The tackling of such questions should bring it about that we no longer prolong an "absurd situation which cannot be pondered on deeply enough precisely by one who is convinced of the usefulness of a Petrine ministry".[21]

[21] H. Küng, *op. cit.*, p. 545.

Translated by David Bourke

James F. McCue

Roman Primacy in the First Three Centuries

IT should be observed at the outset of a discussion of the state of research on the primacy prior to Nicaea, that one's estimate of the importance of the matter is profoundly conditioned by one's theological prepossessions. Within the framework of the prepossessions of, let us say, the *Dictionnaire de théologie catholique*, this is a question on which depends the very existence, or at least the legitimacy of the existence, of Roman Catholicism. On the other hand, within the framework of the suppositions of a work such as Hans Küng's *The Church*, the matter finally has no really decisive importance for the question of the legitimacy of the papacy or of Roman Catholicism. That this should be said seems to me to be important, for it is quite possible and more than possible for the Catholic theological community to go on discussing questions that once were a matter of life and death as though they still had the same importance, whereas the more important issue would seem to be that concerned with the meaning and legitimacy of the claim to ecclesiological and theological unity and continuity across the abyss that separates these two sets of presuppositions.

In order to discuss the origins of a Roman primacy, some sort of definition of what we are talking about must be given. For the purposes of this article I shall mean by "Roman primacy" a claim on the part of the Bishop of Rome to a responsibility and an authority in guiding the Church universal that is beyond that of any other church or bishop.

A characteristic feature of much recent research both into the

New Testament and into early Church history has been the tendency to stress the diversity that one finds in the early Christian communities. Much more is made today of the diversity that seems to have existed within the several local communities—Corinth, Rome, Thessalonica—as well as among these communities. In the past there has been a tendency to assume uniformity at the outset and a gradual simultaneous development throughout the Church universal, the various documents along the way being seen as illustrations of a fairly uniform process. Thus if it could be shown that if Antioch had a clearly differentiated threefold ministry by about A.D. 100, the Church at large could be said to have had such a ministry at that time. If in 180 a bishop in Gaul looked to the churches of apostolic foundation as the norms of genuine Christian faith, then it could be said that by 180 the Church had such a view. Naturally this approach affected the writing of the history of the Roman primacy, and historian-theologians tended to string together a series of rather isolated fragments and to offer these as a kind of outline of the history of the primacy in the entire Church during the period.

We are today much more impressed with the diversities in the early Christian communities; and this quite naturally affects the way in which we treat the question of a Roman primacy. There would today be a fairly widespread acknowledgment that a Roman primacy becomes an unambiguously clear and forceful part of the Roman tradition in the course of the fourth century, that the evidence is sufficiently clear to say that Rome is asserting this primacy by the middle of the third century, but that throughout the whole of the second century neither Rome nor any other church speaks of or acts out a Roman primacy.

I. BISHOPS IN ROME?

So far as can presently be determined, the pattern of events was approximately as follows. Through the entire first century, and perhaps a bit beyond, the church at Rome did not have an episcopal organization in the later sense of the word. We find that at the end of the century (*1 Clement*: A.D. 96–97) that church is ruled by a group of the most esteemed men of the church, and that this pattern is looked upon as going back to apostolic times.

At the same time one finds that this group of leaders is regarded as standing in succession to the apostles, and that to repudiate them *if they have ruled worthily* is to repudiate all that stands behind them. Thus we have expressed quite early at Rome what we might term an apostolic doctrine of the ministry, but the ministry that is of apostolic appointment is presbyterial rather than episcopal.

The authority of the ministry in *1 Clement* is, however, a matter of intra-church order. *Vis-à-vis* other churches *1 Clement* has no theory of ministerial authority. The letter is not proffered as the command or testimony or exhortation of the presbyters of Rome—and of course not of the bishop of Rome—but is rather the statement of the *church* of Rome.

The church at Rome as reflected in *1 Clement* is certainly conscious of a responsibility *vis-à-vis* the church at Corinth. I have argued elsewhere that the responsibility evidenced here does not go beyond what one would expect given the size and prominence of Rome, the likelihood of fairly frequent communication between the two, the shared tradition of a common foundation by Peter and Paul, and the disorders at Corinth.[1] Thus though we may have here evidence of the early stages of a *practice* which in the course of time would lead to claims to primacy, the letter itself does not imply or presuppose such a claim.

Of crucial importance to the later emergence of primatial claims is the Roman tradition, already referred to, that both Peter and Paul were instrumental in the establishment of the Roman church. This is already a source of pride in *1 Clement* and will subsequently be an essential ingredient in Rome's claim to a universal authority.

There is no agreement as to precisely when Rome developed an episcopal form of government. It was certainly later than *1 Clement* and earlier than Irenaeus (*ca.* 180), and it would appear to be much closer to the former date than to the latter. It is difficult to see that any very weighty consequences hang on the decision as to the precise decade of the first half of the second century. The fact that Ignatius of Antioch makes no mention of

---

[1] J. F. McCue, "The Roman Primacy in the Second Century and the Problem of the Development of Dogma", in *Theological Studies*, Vol. 25, No. 2 (June, 1964), pp. 165-9.

a bishop in his letter to the Romans, even though in each of his other letters the episcopacy is a central theme, suggests that it may not have been until after Ignatius (died under Trajan, 98–117) that Rome had a bishop.

II. Regional Structures

Ignatius testifies to the high regard in which the church at Rome was held by other churches, and the fact that it was to Rome that he, the bishop of Antioch, was taken for execution testifies, if testimony is needed, to the importance of the capital city in the life of the time. As I have also tried to show elsewhere, however, Ignatius cannot be interpreted as recognizing a Roman primacy.[2] What makes the interpretation of materials difficult and opens matters up to interminable dispute is the fact that there is already in process of development by Ignatius' time and even somewhat earlier a vaguely defined meta-diocesan organization of the Church. While the local community will still, for a time, remain the dominant reality, there is already taking place a kind of regional structuring of the Church. This will eventually, and especially after Nicaea, conform rather closely to the political divisions of the time;[3] in the second century it is rather a matter of the prominent cities coming to dominate the church life in their region: Antioch, Ephesus, Rome, Carthage, presumably a great many other cities. Given this broad development, it is difficult to know how to interpret, for example, the clear indications that Ignatius considers Rome to be a church having authority. In my opinion such material falls easily enough into a regional-authority pattern, but some writers, especially some of the older Catholic writers, find more in it than that.

An indication that Rome was becoming an even more important and influential church is evidenced by the fact that in the course of the second century many of the leading gnostics came to Rome to try to gain a favourable hearing for their ideas. As to the facts there is no serious disagreement; the question is how these facts bear at all on the question of a Roman primacy. Are

[2] J. F. McCue, *ibid.*, pp. 171–5.
[3] F. Dvornik, *The Idea of Apostolicity in Byzantium and the Legend of the Apostle Andrew* (Cambridge, 1958), pp. 4 *et seq.*

they to be explained as testimony to a widely recognized Roman primacy? I think not. Rather they would seem to arise from the natural importance and centrality of Rome, and thus to be part of a developing practice which would subsequently be transformed into theory in the primatial claims.

Nor does the famed "Paschal Controversy" of the late second century bring us significantly closer to primatial claims.[4] The material here is fairly complex, involving as it does late second-century texts imbedded in an interpretative context provided by Eusebius of Caesarea. On one reading of the material, the controversy is between Rome and Asia Minor over the date for the celebration of Easter, both parties claiming apostolic warrant for their respective traditions. When Asia Minor refuses to submit to Roman dictate, Victor, bishop of Rome, excommunicates the churches of Asia Minor. Elsewhere[5] I have indicated why some maintain that Eusebius seriously misreads his sources, and that the late second-century episode really had to do with an intra-diocesan affair: Victor was commending and then excommunicating Christians at Rome who had come from Asia Minor. If this latter interpretation is correct, and I am inclined to think it is, then the Paschal Controversy is completely irrelevant to the question of primacy. Moreover, even if one accepts the former interpretation, it should be recognized that in the patristic era at least excommunication did not presuppose or imply primatial authority. It was something that could be and often was done among equals.

The only other second-century material of relevance is Irenaeus. Though much of the older Catholic material saw Irenaeus one of the principal early witnesses to Roman primacy, more recent studies have tended to interpret his ecclesiology as multi-centred. He accords a normative function to all the churches of apostolic foundation, and singles out Rome for special consideration because of the impressive character of its apostolic credentials (founded by Peter and Paul), because of its cosmopolitan character, and presumably because in the West it was the only clearly recognizable church of apostolic origin. In Irenaeus we see a *practice* of recourse to Rome as to a doctrinal norm; but the

[4] Eusebius, *H.E.*, 5.23–24.
[5] J. F. McCue, *op. cit.*, pp. 178–84.

Irenaean theory would equate Rome with the other apostolic churches.

III. CONTROVERSY OVER THE PRIMATE

It is not altogether clear at what point in time a Roman bishop first claims primatial authority.[6] In the past, Tertullian's *De pudicitia* (written after 213) was often interpreted as a reaction to such a claim, but it would now be generally agreed that the bishop there accused of claiming an exaggerated authority on the basis of Matthew 16.18 was Agrippinus of Carthage. We therefore come down to the middle of the third century before we find a clear instance of a Roman claim to primacy, and even then the claim is accessible to us only through those opposing it, Cyprian of Carthage and Firmilian of Caesarea.

In Tertullian we have the first unquestionable use of Matthew 16. 18 as a text in support of church authority. Even supposing that it refers to Carthage and not Rome, it is significant that Peter is seen as the key to ecclesiastical authority. The passage in Tertullian runs as follows:

> I now inquire into your opinion, to see from what source you usurp this right to "the Church". If, because the Lord has said to Peter, "Upon this rock I will build My Church", "to thee have I given the keys of the heavenly kingdom", or, "Whatsoever thou shalt have bound or loosed in earth, shall be bound or loosed in the heavens", you therefore presume that the power of binding and loosing has derived to you, that is, to every Church akin to Peter, what sort of man are you, subverting and wholly changing the manifest intention of the Lord, conferring this gift personally akin to Peter?[7]

This would indicate that there was a significant Petrine, though non-primatial, interpretation of authority at Carthage a

---

[6] J. Ludwig, *Die Primatworte Mt 16, 18. 19 in der Altkirchlachen Exergese* (Münster, 1952), finds primatial use of Mt. 16. 18 so indiscriminately that one cannot use the work to answer the question posed here.

[7] "De tua nunc sententia quaero unde hoc ius ecclesiae usurpes. Si quia dixerit Petro Dominus: 'Super hanc Petram aedificabo ecclesiam meam, tibi dedi claves regni caelestis', uel: 'quaecumque alligaueris uel solueris in terra, erunt alligata uel soluta in caelis', idcirco praesumis etud omnem ecclesiam Petri pro-pinquam?" *De Pudicitia*, 21.

generation before Cyprian. It is in the clash between this view and a more exclusively Roman interpretation of Matthew 16. 18 that we first encounter an explicit claim to Roman primacy.

The details of the controversy between Stephen of Rome and Cyprian of Carthage need not be rehearsed here. What is important is that in the course of a controversy over the baptism of schismatics, Stephen claimed that he, as successor of Peter and present occupant of the chair of Peter, shares somehow in Peter's primacy.[8] In Ep. 73 Cypian argues in a way that would seem to concede that the Bishop of Rome is in some way the unique successor to Peter. He points out that Peter, upon whom the Church was built, did not pull rank in his dispute with Paul but rather entered into argument with him; and this Cyprian offers as an example for Stephen to follow.

In the letter of Firmilian to Cyprian,[9] Firmilian speaks of Stephen first as "one who glories in the place of his episcopate and claims to hold the succession of Peter, on whom are placed the foundations of the Church"; and then says that "Stephen . . . proclaims that he possesses the chair of Peter through succession".[10] A remarkable feature of the Firmilian letter is that though the language is quite violent—Stephen is likened to Judas; *"Firmilian iuste indignatur ad hanc tam apertam et manifestam Stephani stultitiam"*—the violence is reserved for his view on the baptism of heretics. The claim to be successor to Peter is not reacted to at all. The *manifesta stultitia* of which Firmilian speaks is for one who claims to be the successor to the foundation of the foundations to accord the status of church to heretical groups. It is not the Petrine claim but the failure to line up to it that outrages Firmilian. Indeed, it would appear that Firmilian did not understand that claim as having any definable jurisdictional consequences. Being successor to Peter in a unique way (i.e., being a successor to the chair of Peter) imposes perhaps special responsibilities but, it would seem, no special power or authority.

From Cyprian, however, we gain the distinct impression that

[8] J. Ludwig, *op. cit.*, pp. 33-4.

[9] Cyprian, *Saint Cyprien Correspondence*, Tome II (Paris, 1961), Ep. 75. 17, p. 301. "Qui sic de episcopatus sui loco gloriatur et se successionem Petri tenere contendit, super quem fundamenta ecclesiae collocata sunt."

[10] Cyprian, *ibid.*, p. 302.. "Stephanus qui per successionem Cathedram Petri habere se praedicat."

Stephen did interpret the Petrine succession as conferring authority. Such at least is the simplest interpretation of the inferred revision of the text of chapter four of *De ecclesiae catholicae unitate*. Here, after first articulating his theory of the Petrine basis of the episcopacy in a way that could be taken to support primatial claim, Cyprian revises his original text so as to make clearer the essentially equal status of all the bishops in relationship to Peter. It is difficult to imagine what could have occasioned this revision unless it be that during the time separating the two versions Cyprian was faced with Roman primatial claims.

IV. ROME'S PRIMATE

If we focus our attention exclusively on events or on documents that have, or have been thought to have, a primatial meaning, we are liable to overlook developments that are quite important to the shaping of Roman primacy. Thus in the third century Rome was frequently called upon to intervene in intra-diocesan disputes in a number of Western churches. When, early in the fourth century, the Donatist controversy grew up in North Africa, it was Rome that was the principal (albeit not the only) church called upon to render judgment. Gradually Rome developed into the undisputed premier see of the West, and the one which dealt with the East on behalf of the West.

It is in the fourth century, and the latter part of the fourth century, that Rome clearly and with some persistence lays claim to primacy. The third canon of Constantinople I, an essentially Eastern affair, grants to Rome first place in the Church, but claims for Constantinople second place on the grounds that Constantinople is the new Rome. The basis on which the Easterners would seem to be acting would be the assumption that the church organizations should parallel the organization of society. Rome would thus be the premier church, but not because it derived any special authority or status from its Petrine origin.[11]

Rome, on the other hand, claimed an altogether different basis for its position. We may presume that the Petrine-primatial tradition was alive at Rome continuously from at least the time of Stephen; but it is the popes from the time of Constantinople I—

---

[11] F. Dvornik, *op. cit.*, pp. 39–41.

Damascus, Siricius, Innocent, Zosimus, Boniface and finally Leo
—that forcefully reiterate the idea that the Bishop of Rome, *qua*
successor to Peter, is the principal bishop, possessor of *the* apostolic see, and that apart from him one is outside the Church.
This theme becomes more central between Constantinople I and
Chalcedon in part owing to the Church's need for some kind of
organizational unity given the Church's still relatively new status
as the religion of the Empire.

The effort of emperors to play the role of *episcopus episcoporum*; and the ruinous consequences of this in the fourth and
fifth centuries, made more urgent the problem of church organization and authority; made more attractive, more relevant Rome's
Petrine-primatial claims. At the same time, the clearer statement
of Eastern bishops of the basically political basis of Rome's leadership, together with the rival claims of a rapidly developing Constantinople, reinforced the Roman claim that it was the Petrine
foundation of the Roman Church and nothing else that established its primacy.

This claim, of course, was Roman in origin, and initially seems
to have been part only of the Roman tradition. It was gradually
accepted in the West as the basis for Rome's already very real
leadership. In the terms in which it was formulated by Rome it
was never widely accepted in the East. The church at Rome was
entitled to a kind of universal primacy owing to its location in
the capital of the world; but this primacy, different in basis from
what Rome claimed, did not have the consequences that Rome
assumed. Only if one already presupposed the Roman interpretation to be the correct one could one make the Roman witness
the decisive one; only if one granted Roman primacy in the sense
claimed by Siricius or the *Decretum Galesianum* could the Roman
tradition be taken to settle the issue in a divided Church. In the
patristic era the issue was never settled in a generally satisfactory
way.

Wilhelm de Vries

Theoretical and Practical Renewals of the Primacy of Rome

1. *The Development after Constantine*

UNTIL the time of Constantine, Christians had, of course, been persecuted. From then onwards, however, Christianity quickly became the official religion of the Empire and it was only to be expected that the bishop of the ancient capital of the Empire would come to occupy a somewhat different position. This does not mean that the primacy of Rome only in fact originated after Constantine or that we should look for the decisive reason for the pre-eminence of Rome in the political supremacy of that city. None the less, it is an undeniable fact that Rome developed, in a way that could hardly have been anticipated, towards a position of primacy after Constantine.

I. The Claims of Rome

In this article, I shall first outline very briefly this development from the point of view of the expectations of Rome and then go on to discuss the extent to which the Roman idea of primacy in fact prevailed in the West and in the East. It will, of course, be obvious that I shall be able to do no more, in such a short article, than simply to provide a few guide-lines.

The first idea which emerged more prominently after Constantine than before this turning-point in the history of the Church was that the apostle Peter himself continued to live in the bishop of Rome and that, for this reason, this bishop should have the authority of Peter. This idea was expressed, for example, by Damasus (366-384)[1] and in the well-known declaration on primacy which the presbyter Philip, representing Celestine I, made at the Council of Ephesus (431).[2] Leo the Great (440-461) provided a more precise juridical definition for the idea of succession, according to which the bishop of Rome was to be regarded as the (unworthy) successor and heir of Peter.[3]

Rome's claim to authority over the whole Church emerged from this idea of legal succession. This claim was made by Innocent I (401-417), who accompanied it with Paul's "anxiety for all the churches" (*sollicitudo omnium ecclesiarum*, 2 Cor. 11. 28),[4] a phrase which was to be repeated again and again throughout the history of the Church, and reiterated by Celestine I.[5] Leo the Great claimed, as Peter's heir, the *plenitudo potestatis* in the Church.[6] This is, of course, a key concept and one which was taken up again, for example, by the First Vatican Council.[7] Leo also advanced the remarkable argument that the apostles had received their full powers, not directly from the Lord, but rather through Peter.[8] Although he recognized the distinctive legal powers of the bishops,[9] he regarded only his vicar in Thessalonica as his functionary who shared in the fullness of papal power.[10] He did not believe that all the bishops participated in the fullness of the power of the pope. This idea was first expressed in the ninth century, in the Pseudo-Isidorian Decretals.[11] Later, at the Second Council of Lyons in 1274, it was again expressed in the *Professio fidei Michaelis Palaeologi*.[12]

If the fullness of power in the Church should be accorded to the bishop of Rome, then it must follow that Rome is the *head*

[1] The following abbreviations are used in this article: *ACO = Acta Conciliorum Oecumenicorum*, ed. E. Schwartz (Berlin and Leipzig, 1927 ff.); Congar = Y. Congar, *L'Ecclésiologie du haut moyen-âge* (Paris, 1968); Heiler = F. Heiler, *Altkirchliche Autonomie und päpstlicher Zentralismus* (Munich, 1941); Hinschius = *Decretales Pseudo-Isidorianae*, ed. P. Hinschius (Leipzig, 1863); Mansi = J. D. Mansi, *Sacrorum Conciliorum nova et amplissima collectio*, IV ff. (Florence, 1740 ff.); *PL* = Migne, *Patrologia Latina*. Note 1 refers to *PL* 13, 370 B.

[2] Mansi, IV, 1295-1296; *ACO*, I, I, 3, 60.
[3] *Sermo*, III, 4, *PL*, 54, 147 A.   [5] *PL* 50, 485 A.
[4] *Epistola* 30, *PL* 20, 590 A.   [6] *Epistola* 14, *PL* 54, 671 B.
[7] Denzinger and Schönmetzer, 3064.   [8] *Sermo* IV, 2, *PL*, 54, 149.
[9] *Epistola* 10, 2, *PL*, 54, 650 A.   [10] *Epistola* 14, 1, *PL*, 54, 671 B.
[11] Hinschius, 712, VII.   [12] Denzinger and Schönmetzer, 861.

of all the churches. This idea had already been expressed in the fifth century by Boniface I (418–422).[13] Leo took it up again and defined it more precisely in his five Christmas sermons.[14] The legates representing him at the Council of Chalcedon in 451 put forward this view[15] and concluded that the bishop of Rome was either the "bishop of all the churches"[16] or else the "bishop of the universal Church".[17] The Fathers of the Council, however, did *not* accept the bishop of Rome as the "universal bishop" or the "universal pope" and Gregory the Great (590–604) firmly rejected this title, which could so easily be misunderstood, because it could, in his opinion, lead to an infringement of the rights of the bishops.[18]

The "bishop of the universal Church" is able to exclude some-one from the whole Church. Communion with him is essential for membership of the Church. In other words, Rome is the *decisive centre* of the *communio* of the Church. This claim was made by Celestine I in the first century in the controversy with Nestorius.[19]

In excluding Nestorius from the universal Church because of heresy, Celestine was claiming full *teaching authority* and the absolute character of this authority emerges clearly from the fact that the sentence passed against Nestorius by Celestine and his Roman synod was regarded as the "judgment of Jesus Christ himself".[20] It is, however, important to note here that this papal decision was at the same time a *synodal* decision. This was un-doubtedly the custom in Rome during the first thousand years of Christian history.[21] It is open to question whether a genuine right to share in such decisions was accorded to the Roman synod or not. Rome was reluctant to recognize the synodal prin-ciple at the level of the universal Church. Celestine, for example, instructed his legates at the Council of Ephesus not to permit

---

[13] *Epistola* 14, PL, 20, 777.
[14] PL, 54, 141–56; see *Sermo* 82, PL, 54, 422–4.
[15] ACO, II, I, 1, 65; Mansi, VI, 580.
[16] ACO, II, I, 2, 93; Mansi, VII, 9.
[17] ACO, II, I, 2, 141; Mansi, VII, 135–6.   [18] PL, 77, 933 C.
[19] ACO, I, II, 12; Mansi, IV, 1036 A.
[20] ACO, I, II, 22; Mansi, IV, 1292 D.
[21] For example, Leo the Great: PL, 54, 827; Martin I: Mansi, X, 1154; Agatho: Mansi, XI, 294 D.

any discussion,[22] although it is, of course, true that he left the
Fathers of the Council *formally* free to give their consent to his
decision if it seemed to them to further the good of the whole
Church.[23] The pope's letter to the synod is in itself a hymn of
praise to the principle of collegiality.[24] Leo, on the other hand,
demanded categorically that the Council of Chalcedon should
accept without discussion his so-called Tome to Flavian, which,
in his view, provided a decisive and final answer to the question
of faith.[25] Pope Agatho (678–681) also behaved in a similar way
later towards the Third Council of Constantinople (680–681), as
did Adrian I (772–795) towards the Second Council of Nicaea
(787).[26]

Leo certainly claimed unconditional teaching authority, but he
also stressed his agreement with all the bishops and even with
all the members of the whole Church. He spoke as the author-
ized witness of the faith of the whole Church.[27] He based his
claim to possess full teaching authority in the Church on the
help of the Holy Spirit and the succession of Peter.[28] Any idea
that his authority had been, as it were, given to him democrati-
cally from below was quite alien to him. On the contrary, it was
intimately connected with his office as the heir of Peter.

This *plenitudo potestatis* in the Church, which was claimed
as early as the fifth century for the papacy by Leo the Great, includes not only full teaching authority, but also the *full power
to make laws in the Church*. Gelasius I (492–496) was the
first pope to add his decretals and those of his predecessors to the
synodal collections of canons. He attributed a similar legislative
power to these as well as to the synodal resolutions.[29]

The papal decretals have since then formed an integral part
of the canon law of the Western Church. They are valid in
themselves and, in the opinion of Rome, have no need to be
received by the Church.[30] The popes too have always regarded
themselves as bound by the conciliar canons and they have

---

[22] *ACO*, I, I, 3, 58; Mansi, IV, 1289 C.
[23] *ACO*, I, II, 24; Mansi, IV, 1288 B.
[24] *ACO*, I, II, 22–4; Mansi, IV, 1284–8.
[25] *PL*, 54, 937–9.   [26] Mansi, XI, 294 D, E; Mansi, XII, 1086.
[27] *PL*, 54, 891–2; see also *op. cit.*, 783.   [28] *Op. cit.*, 930, 821.
[29] Congar, p. 136.   [30] Congar, p. 380.

always promised on election to respect these canons and the practices of the whole Church.[31]

In addition to this legislative power, Rome has also, for many centuries, claimed to have *control over the synods* in which ecclesiastical laws are made. Innocent I (402–417) insisted that the *causae minores* discussed at local synods had to be referred for final judgment to Rome.[32] Leo the Great's legate at the Council of Chalcedon, Lucentius, accused Dioscorus of having dared to hold a synod without the authority of the Holy See. This should never have been allowed, the legate maintained, and ought never to have taken place.[33] Acting on the Petrine authority invested in him, Leo the Great rescinded Canon 28, which had been accepted by the Council of Chalcedon.[34] The Holy See also annulled the synod which had bestowed on Archbishop John Nesteutes of Constantinople the title of "ecumenical patriarch".[35] At the Roman synod of 864, Nicholas I (858–867) proclaimed the principle that no *concilium generale* could be held without the permission of Rome.[36] The concept *concilium generale* was, moreover, left so vague that almost any council in any region could be regarded as such. The Pseudo-Isidorian Decretals, which originated in France round about the middle of the ninth century and which Nicholas I regarded as authentic and used, laid down that no synod of any kind could be held without the permission of Rome.[37]

This, then, is very briefly indeed the main outline of the development of the primacy of Rome in the post-Constantinian Church. What we have to consider now is *which of these claims or which part or parts of them*, made by popes since the time of Constantine, *are based on divine law and which are not*. The fact that a pope makes a claim does not necessarily mean that he has any right to do so on the basis of the Petrine office founded by Christ and handed on to him. In the course of his-

---

[31] *Liber Diurnus Romanorum Pontificum*, ed. T. E. Ab Sickel (Vindobonae, 1889), pp. 91–2, formula no. 83.
[32] *PL*, 20, 473.   [33] *ACO*, II, I, 1, 65; Mansi, VI, 581.
[34] *Epistola*, 105, 3, *PL*, 54, 1000
[35] *Acta Romanorum Pontificum a S. Clemente ad Coelestinum*, III, Vol. I, in *Pontificia Commissio ad redigendum codicem Iuris Canonici Orientalis*, Fontes, Series III, Vol. I (Vatican, 1943), p. 470, note 249.
[36] Mansi, XIV, 686 B.   [37] Hinschius 19, VIII.

tory, there have undeniably been legitimate claims made by popes which were exaggerated and conditioned by the prevailing historical situation and which cannot be upheld any longer to-day. What is much more important if we are to make a true distinction between divine and human law in this case is the reception of these claims by the Church as a whole. Our question therefore is: To what extent was the theory formulated by the popes accepted in the West and in the East and to what extent was it realized in practice?

II. Accepted by the Church?

Before attempting to answer this question, a short outline must be provided of the *putting into practice of papal primacy* in the West. The development, which took place over many centuries, basically amounted to an extension of the originally very limited sphere of influence of the Roman metropolitan to the whole of the Western Christian world. In the West as in the East of Europe and elsewhere, there were originally many auto-nomous churches, in which the influence of Rome was, despite the theoretical claims made by the popes, in fact very slight. It is, of course, obvious that political circumstances also played a very important part in this development. In Italy, Milan, Aquileia and Ravenna were the rivals of Rome. The rise of these cities in the Church was conditioned by political factors[38]—Milan and Aquileia were for a time the residences of the emperor in the fourth century and Ravenna was the emperor's residence at the beginning of the fifth century and, from the middle of the sixth century onwards, the seat of the Byzantine exarch.

The African church had, from the earliest times, possessed considerable autonomy. The Council of Carthage (418) had even forbidden any appeal to be made to Rome.[39] The church of the Merovingian Empire was only very loosely associated with Rome. The same applies to the church of the Spanish Visigoths, who did not become Catholic until the year 589. The synods that were held at this time in Gaul and Spain were under the control, not of the pope, but of the kings.[40] The Celtic churches in

[38] See Heiler, *Altchristliche Autonomie, op. cit.*
[39] Mansi, III, 822.   [40] See Congar, p. 133.

Britain, Scotland and Ireland were also very independent from the very beginning.

There are various reasons for the enormous spread of the Roman sphere of influence later. Political reasons played a particularly important part, of course, but so did, for example, the missionary activity in England and Germany which emanated from Rome. After the collapse of the national monarchy in 711 as a result of the Moorish invasions, the Spanish church became increasingly Roman. In France, it was the policy of Pepin and later of Charlemagne to reinforce the influence of Rome in order to strengthen the unity of the Empire. The influence of Rome was also furthered by the personal attitude of Boniface (+754). In 722, he made a bishop's oath to Gregory II which was very similar to that made by the suburbicarian bishops.[41] Augustine, whom Gregory the Great sent to evangelize England, established his missionary church in very close association with Rome. The English mission also influenced the Celtic churches and brought them more closely into association with Rome.

Nicholas I, who knew how to break the power of the metropolitans, made an essential and personal contribution to the extension of the influence of the Roman metropolitan throughout the whole of the Western Church. He and John VIII (872–882), who was pope shortly after the pontificate of Nicholas, gave the pallium its juridical significance as a sign of participation in the full power of the pope. The supra-diocesan full powers of the metropolitans were in this way interpreted as privileges bestowed by the pope.[42]

This development did not, of course, take place without fundamental opposition on the part of the metropolitans. An important figure in this controversy was Hincmar, who was bishop of Rheims from 845 until 882. Hincmar took a very positive attitude towards the primacy of divine law, but did not regard the unity of the Church as a pontifical monarchy[43] and believed that primacy should be exercised with the respect that was due to the structures of the Church and divine order. Legal decisions taken by the popes were, in his opinion, not simply and solely valid

[41] Heiler, p. 230.   [42] Congar, p. 205.
[43] Congar, p. 166 ff.

when they were accepted by the whole Church." Many church-men, including Gerbert of Aurillac, who later became Pope Sylvester II (999–1003), also believed that the bishop of Rome lost the Petrine privilege if he lost sight of its *aequitas.*[45] The Church was above all not a monarchy, in which everything stemmed from the head.[46]

The Roman idea of primacy in the Church made *very much less progress in the East* than in the West. One part of Europe which is usually known as the "East" was, however, under the supreme authority of Rome until 732. This was western Illyricum. Popes Damasus I and Siricius (384–399) were able to instal a vicar there, in Thessalonica, towards the end of the fourth century and this vicar governed the church in Illyricum in their name.[47] The patriarchs of Constantinople, Alexandria, Antioch and Jerusalem, however, became more and more autonomous.[48]

In contrast to the excessive emphasis placed by Rome on the monarchical principle, the Eastern Church stressed the principle of collegiality. In the Eastern tradition, decisions concerning faith and discipline which affected the whole Church could, normally at least, only be made by the whole college of bishops with the pope at its head. The history of the ecumenical councils during the first Christian millennium provides striking evidence of this fact.[49]

Even though the Eastern Church has quite often acknowledged the succession of the bishop of Rome in the Petrine office, it has never accepted a mystical identification of the bishop of Rome with the apostle Peter, in the way in which the Western Church has frequently done. The acclamation of the Fathers of

[44] Congar, p. 175.
[45] *Lettres de Gerbert,* ed. J. Havet (Paris, 1889), *Epistola* 192, p. 180; see also Congar, p. 184.
[46] Congar, p. 183.   [47] Siricius: *PL,* 13, 1148.
[48] See G. de Vries, "La S. Sede ed i patriarcati cattolici d'Oriente", in *Or. Christ. Per.* 27 (1961), pp. 316 ff.
[49] See W. de Vries, "Die Struktur der Kirche gemäss dem Konzil von Chalkedon", in *Or. Christ. Per.* 35 (1969), pp. 63–122; "Die Struktur der Kirche gemäss dem III. Konzil von Konstantinopel", in *Volk Gottes. Festgabe für Josef Höfer* (Freiburg, 1967), pp. 262–85; "Die Struktur der Kirche gemäss dem II. Konzil von Nicäa", in *Or. Chr. Per.* 33 (1967), pp. 47–71; "Die Struktur der Kirche gemäss dem IV. Konzil von Konstantinopel", in *Archivum Hist. Pont.* 6 (1968), pp. 7–42.

the Council of Chalcedon: "Peter has spoken through Leo" cannot be thought of as placing Leo on the same level as the apostle.[50]

The Eastern Church did not recognize the power of Rome to formulate unilaterally legal norms which would apply to the whole of the Church. The papal decretals do not, for example, figure at all among the legal sources included in the Trullanum of 691.[51] The fact that all *causae maiores* should of necessity be decided in Rome has never been accepted as valid in the East, nor have the principles of *plenitudo potestatis* and *Suprema Sedes a nemine iudicatur*.[52] What is more, the Eastern Church has never regarded Rome as the only valid centre of Church *communio*.[53]

If we were to take the Eastern tradition of Christianity quite seriously, we might find that it could help us in the West to tone down some of our more exaggerated ideas about the primacy of Rome and thus to make it a little more plausible to the Church as a whole.

[50] W. de Vries, "Die Struktur der Kirche gemäss dem Konzil von Chalkedon", *op. cit.*, pp. 102 ff.

[51] Mansi, XI, 940–1.

[52] See P. L'Huillier, "Collégialité et primauté", in *Collégialité Episcopale* (Paris, 1965), p. 343.

[53] See W. de Vries, "Die Struktur der Kirche gemäss dem Konzil von Chalkedon", *op. cit.*, p. 120; "Die Struktur der Kirche gemäss dem IV. Konzil von Konstantinopel", *op. cit.*, pp. 32 ff.; for the whole subject, see also Y. Congar, *L'Eglise de saint Augustin à l'époque moderne* (Paris, 1970).

Translated by David Smith

Horst Fuhrmann

Theoretical and Practical Renewals of the Primacy of Rome

2. *From the Early Middle Ages until the Gregorian Reform*

I. The Way towards a Church State

THE contribution made during the Middle Ages towards a more pronounced primacy of Rome within the Church would at first sight seem to be very small. That exemplary pope of the medieval Church, Gregory I (590–604), gave a distinct shape to the image of the bishop of Rome which was to have a strong influence in the future—the bishop as the servant and shepherd of his flock. It was Gregory who first called himself the *servus servorum Dei* and who regarded missionary work as his central task as the bishop of Rome. He added hardly anything more to the principles outlined by Leo I (440–469) concerning the idea of papal primacy, unless, of course, we accept what the liberal Protestant historian Johannes Haller († 1947) has said about his missionizing of the northern European peoples. In his conversion of the Anglo-Saxons, Haller claimed, Gregory was responsible for bringing about a radical historical change in the papacy. He aroused devotion among the northern converts to the figure of Peter and thus succeeded in placing the reservation of faith on the Roman primacy in jurisdiction.

The figure of Peter as the manly prince of the apostles and the keeper of the gates of heaven met with a powerful response among the Germanic tribes and made them turn resolutely towards Rome. When Haller's book was first published, one reviewer asked whether the papacy was really, as this author claimed, a "Germanic invention". Of course, Haller's argument is hardly tenable in this massive form, but it cannot easily be disputed that the Roman Anglo-Saxon mission of Willibald and of Winfrith (Boniface, † 754) brought the Franks closer to Rome and, what is more, did this at a time when Rome was beginning to break away from the pressure and protection of Constantinople.

The seventh century with its dogmatic conflicts between Rome and Constantinople was followed by a definitive break, brought about particularly by the question of the legitimacy of worshipping images. The pope sought the protection of the Franks in an attempt to escape both from the imminent danger of being executed by the Byzantine emperor and from the constant threat from the Lombards. Pope Zachary (741–752) advocated and morally justified the fall of the Merovingian dynasty and the establishment of the Carlovingian monarchy in 751 and this new alliance enabled the papacy to wait for a suitable opportunity to set up a church state. This opportunity presented itself after the successful raids made by the Franks against the Lombards and the ultimate downfall of the Lombardic empire in 774.

What emerged from this situation, we may assume, was the "Constantinian donation". This had originated as an ideal, but did not become a reality until the High and Late Middle Ages. According to this donation, the Emperor Constantine († 337) had granted to Pope Sylvester I (314–335) a position equal to that of the emperor and had ceded to him the western part of his lands. In fact, the pope had simply assumed the transitory privileges of a Greek king and these privileges were later handed over to Charlemagne (768–814) when the imperial idea was revived in the West. When Charlemagne was crowned emperor in 800, apparently to his great surprise, he was placed at once in the difficult situation of a Western emperor in competition with the Eastern, Byzantine emperor, while his imperial position had been established by the papacy. In his view, the bishop of Rome was really little more than the most important bishop in his empire and the church state was simply a privileged territory within the whole territory that he ruled.

II. CENTRALIZED AUTHORITY

During the reign of Charlemagne's successors, a gradual

change came about in the relationship between the papacy and the empire. The various agreements drawn up between the Carlovingian rulers and the popes and the different versions of the imperial privileges bear witness to this change. Within the context of his coronation, the emperor drew up a charter for the pope, guaranteeing to protect the Roman Church and to respect its possessions. The papacy rose to a particularly high point in the Carlovingian era during the pontificate of Nicholas I (858–867). He called King Lothair II (855–869) sharply to account, for example, because of his divorce and remarriage, thus constraining the secular ruler of Western Christendom to respect the judgment of the Church and especially of its leader, the pope, by treating him as a sinful member of the Church. At the same time, Nicholas worked to make the doctrine of the two powers outlined by Gelasius I (492–496) a living reality by securing freedom from the influence of the State in the affairs of the Church. He was unshakeably convinced of the importance of the hierarchical structure of the Church with the pope at its summit and made constant efforts to subdue the Frankish bishops, who were striving towards autonomy, to his rule and to make all important judicial decisions himself.

This centralization of authority in himself as pope was, of course, seriously criticized and he was accused of behaving like an emperor. But he was so determined to put his view of the supreme value of the papacy at the head of the Church's hierarchy into practice that he forced the Bulgarian Church, which had hitherto been quite prepared to join the Western Church, into an alliance with Constantinople. Even more important for the future of the Church, however, were Nicholas's proclamations concerning the position of Rome in the matter of jurisdiction. Most of the elements in his idea of the primacy of the pope were not, of course, new. What was new was the clarity with which they were expressed. It is therefore not without good reason that Nicholas I is mentioned more than perhaps any other pope since Gregory I (590–604) in the collections of Gregorian jurisprudence and in the medieval "canon law" of Gratian's Decree (*ca.* 1140).

What precisely did Nicholas I mean by papal supremacy? We may summarize his view very briefly by saying that, by stressing what Congar has called the "juristical authority" of Rome, he insisted that the effectiveness of any decision in the Church as a whole depended ultimately on the pope's share in that decision. Conciliar resolutions, for example, were not valid until they had been ratified by Rome. Rome could conduct all legal proceedings and was the supreme court of appeal in the Christian world. The pope was able to proclaim new laws whenever the occasion demanded it. Rome was "spiritually" present everywhere in the Church.

It is probable that it was during the pontificate of Nicholas I that the so-called Pseudo-Isidorian Decretals—forgeries which Haller called the "greatest trick played in the history of the world"— came to Rome from Franconia. These documents emphasize above all the primacy of the pope in the matter of jurisdiction, especially for the purpose of protecting suffragan bishops effectively against the decisions made by synods and metropolitan bishops. Rome did not, however, as Ignaz von Döllinger has commented, seize on these decretals "eagerly and at once", for the simple reason that Nicholas I did not really need them—he was already sufficiently convinced of the importance of papal primacy. But the fact that many of his decisions were so close in spirit to statements contained in the forgeries does indicate that Nicholas's attitude may have helped to further the spread of their influence later in the Church. This influence was, however, not really felt until the eleventh century, when it permeated the Church by way of the various collections of ecclesiastical laws.

III. PAPAL PRIVILEGE BREAKS THE CANON OF THE WHOLE CHURCH

"The Roman Church alone was founded by the Lord"; "it is the sole privilege of the pope to make new laws when the need arises"; "the Roman Church has always been and will always be free to formulate new laws and to find new remedies to counteract excrescences whenever they appear and no man is permitted to reject those laws as ineffectual". The author of these statements was Hildebrand, Pope Gregory VII (1073–1085) and they are contained in his *Dictatus Papae*. Gregory refused to be bound by what his predecessors had laid down and saw no harm in condemning them for having been negligent in

many matters. More than any other pope before him, he insisted on a primacy in jurisdictional questions, in other words,
on the universal validity of apostolic laws and decisions.

On the other hand, however, he also expressed in many different ways his conviction that he was, in this, only following in
the footsteps of the Church Fathers and continuing their work.
Peter Damian († 1072) declared that Gregory had earnestly
asked him, before his election to the papacy, to examine the
"resolutions and the history" of the bishops of Rome and to set
out in detail those aspects which were the special province of the
authority of the apostolic see. Gregory was convinced that jurisdiction was central in the life of the Roman Church, whether
that law took the form of an earlier legal statute or of a new en-
actment. It was this attitude which gave rise to the frequent
declaration that the man who was not in agreement with and
did not obey the Roman Church was heretical.

Gregory VII was not a jurist himself, however. There is no
evidence in any of the numerous letters that he wrote (there
are about four hundred of these) that he had a profound knowledge of the law or that he had been educated as a canon lawyer.
He clearly did not base his actions on a seriously considered
knowledge of legal principles or on a desire to administer the
law. On the contrary, he acted as a consequence of deep religious
conviction and of a supreme consciousness of his Christian mission. He saw himself, as I have hinted above, as a man who was
continuing the work of the early Fathers of the Church: "Even
though I could, if it were necessary, present the Church with my
own decisions, this is not what I am doing. I am rather renew-
ing the statutes of the Fathers." He regarded his decrees as
parallel to the principles laid down by the early Church. He
could amplify these, but he did not forgo his papal privilege if
he did not.

Gregory was the guardian of tradition in the Church. He preserved that tradition, but at the same time believed that he also
had the authority to cancel out anything detrimental to the life
of the Church that might have crept into that tradition, even if
what was involved was an old custom. Quoting Cyprian in this
context, he declared: "Christ did not say, I am custom. What he
said was, I am the truth", and Gregory had the right, by virtue

of his divine consecration as the bishop of Rome, to decide what this truth might be as well as outstanding holiness as a man and as a bishop. In this way, an a-historical element was added to the bond with tradition—Pope Gregory VII was able, wherever he believed it to be necessary, to free himself from the tradition of the Church and to formulate new norms based on Christian truth.

He was very consistent. He revoked the privileges of his predecessors whenever they seemed to him to be contrary to the "statutes of the Fathers". Every pope, bound to the tradition of the Church and to apostolic truth, was free in his own decisions —as Gregory's devoted follower, Bernold of Constance († 1100) said, "One of the privileges of the apostolic see is that it is the judge of the Church's canons and decrees". A new phrase became common in the papal documents relating to the Gregorian reform. It was "subject to the authority of the apostolic see" and its primary meaning was that the apostolic see did not intend to part definitively with any of its rights or privileges. This clause, which was inserted by Pope Gregory VII into the privileges with special reference to them, was applied without distinction from the eleven forties onwards, that is from the time of Celestine II (1143–1144). Anyone who is able to quote such rights to make reservations of this kind should do so in this case, where early statutes stood in the way and laws that had hitherto prevailed had to be repealed. The primacy of the pope in jurisdictional matters remained firmly bound to the principle that papal privilege breaks the canon of the whole Church. And, on the other hand, from the point of view of the validity of the law, the principle also applied that effective law is everything that is in agreement with the apostolic see.

IV. THE JURIST POPES

Wishing, like Christ himself, who also made himself subject to the law and did so to give an example to others, the popes submitted of their own free will to the existing laws of the Church. On the other hand, however, they also "frequently showed, by their mandates, decisions, decrees and different actions, that they were the lords and makers of laws". These words were written by Gratian, a Camaldolite monk from Bologna, who has been called the "father of ecclesiastical jurisprudence", in his decree, the *Decretum Gratiani*, which was soon to become the only valid and universally accepted collection of earlier sources of canon law. For Gratian, papal primacy was above all a primacy in questions of jurisdiction. This new legislative principle of the bishop of Rome noted by Gratian—namely that papal privilege breaks the canon of the whole Church—resulted in a flood of decretals so great that even those well acquainted with ecclesiastical law at the time groaned. Bishop Stephen of Tournai († 1203) complained, round about the year 1200, to the pope about the "impenetrable forest of papal decretals" in which "the old sacred canons" were "rejected, disapproved of and cast aside".

From the middle of the twelfth century onwards, the jurist who had specialized in legal studies had an established place in the pattern of papal legislation by decretals. The whole leadership and guidance of the Christian world might even have begun to assume the form of an activity conducted mainly by lawyers if a pope brought up into the contemplative tradition—the papal image favoured by Bernard of Clairvaux († 1153)—had not proved convincing both theoretically and in the figure of Eugenius III (1145–1153), a Cistercian himself and a disciple of Bernard.

The first of the jurist popes, however, followed soon after Eugenius. This was Alexander III (1159–1181), who had, before he became pope, taught law at Bologna and had been chancellor of the Roman Church. His pontificate was characterized by a deep conviction that he was the supreme legal authority in the Church. He reigned for twenty-two years and was, in that time, responsible for a fifth of all the known papal letters and documents issued up to the turn of the century—and more than a thousand decretals were promulgated by the papacy during the twelfth century. Certainly, only a specialist could have found his way through this "impenetrable forest".

For many years, men who had almost without exception received a legal training were appointed, after Alexander III, to the papacy. To take this list of jurist popes only to the beginning of the thirteenth century, we may name Urban III

(1185–1187), Gregory VIII (1187), Clement III (1187–1191), Celestine III (1191–1198) and Innocent III (1198–1216). Two other jurist popes who also formed peaks in the papacy of the Middle Ages were the hierocrats Innocent IV (1243–1254) and Boniface VIII (1294–1303).

The Gregorian reform began as a predominantly ecclesiological movement. It culminated, however, in a primacy of Rome that was above all juristical and hierarchical. Gregory VII's spirituality was entirely directed towards ensuring that the Roman Church should carry out its saving task, but his reform initiated a development which ultimately resulted in a continued attempt on the part of successive jurist popes to regulate by law the various forms and expressions of life in the Church. Alexander III and the popes who succeeded him were the consequence of Gregory VII.

Translated by David Smith

Emmanuel Lanne

The Papacy and the Reformation

1. *To what Extent is Roman Primacy unacceptable to the Eastern Churches?*

THERE is no doubt that the primacy of Rome is the principal obstacle standing in the way of a reconstituted unity with the Orthodox Churches. Other differences are not negligible, particularly the thousand-year debate on whom the Holy Spirit proceeds from, and the two Marian dogmas, but the Orthodox regard these as essentially "papist innovations" which stem from the pretensions of the See of Rome.

There are in fact very many Orthodox, including those best disposed towards the Roman Catholic Church, who would regard the two definitions of 1870 as *heresy in the strict sense of the term.* That is to say, they regard them as a serious innovation in matters concerning the faith, in contradiction to revelation, and in particular to the general teaching of the Fathers. Catholic apologetic has tried, for the last hundred years, to show that the definitions of Vatican I were in keeping with the general lines of tradition, and has looked to the writings of the Greek Fathers in particular to support this contention. But it must be objectively recognized that the supports found are few and of little weight. In any case, they failed to convince those they were aimed at.

I. THE DOGMA OF VATICAN I IS UNACCEPTABLE

The dogma of Vatican I contains two quite distinct elements: primacy of jurisdiction and personal infallibility. While it is the second of these that has met with most resistance in the West,

for the Orthodox the question of immediate and universal jurisdiction seems the more pressing, since infallibility is seen as a
mere corollary of this. There is adequate basis for this view in
fact, since historically it has been the claim to jurisdiction that
has been the main burden on the Christian East, particularly
since the Crusades, whose terrible consequences have never been
forgotten in the East. The consequences of the doctrine of infallibility have been minimal in practice, since Catholics have
been debating the limits of the doctrine and the conditions in
which it can be exercised ever since Vatican I. With the primacy
of jurisdiction, though, the case is very different: even if Vatican
I in fact went little further than the Council of Florence in defining the extent of this primacy, the logical consequence of the
three canons that sanction it, and the anathemas hurled against
those who would deny it, is to set up a series of apparently insurmountable obstacles between the two Churches.

1. *Primacy of Jurisdiction*

The first canon relating to the jurisdiction of the Roman
Pontiff affirms the primacy of Peter; this is stated to be a primacy
of true and personal jurisdiction, received directly and immediately by the apostle from the Lord himself (DS 3055).

The Eastern tradition has always recognized a certain primacy
of Peter among the Twelve, and there are ancient texts that support this reading very strongly. But it nevertheless remains true
that Western thought reads more into them than does the
Eastern tradition. Besides this, some Orthodox today have will-
ingly embraced the questioning of the extent of Peter's authority
undertaken by Protestant exegetes. Some would like to oppose a
primacy of John to the primacy of Peter, and, in any case, there
can be no doubt that the Greek patristic tradition hardly favours
the Roman interpretation of the *logion* in Matthew 16. 18.

The second canon (DS 3058) has also met with very strong
criticism. It affirms that it is by divine right that Peter has successors in the primacy and that these successors are the Roman
Pontiffs. All the rest follows from this canon.

The Orthodox, on the other hand, hold that *Rome is not the
only See of Peter*. Other Churches have claims to this succession,
even if Rome holds a special place. But even more important is

the argument stemming from St Cyprian's teaching that *each bishop in his own See* can in some way claim to be the successor of Peter. So if some Church has a higher authority, and even a superior jurisdiction to others, it owes it not to a privileged succession from the apostle Peter, but to decisions of the councils at most, or to a general fact of tradition, which may well go back to the earliest times, as in the case of Rome.

The definition of the primacy itself (DS 3060) and the canon sanctioning it (DS 3064) are totally inadmissible for the Orthodox, and even incomprehensible. For the Roman Pontiff's primatial power of jurisdiction to be called truly episcopal—that is to say ordinary and immediate over absolutely all the faithful and all pastors—constitutes the scandal of what they call "papism". To understand the full implications of this, it should be remembered that this doctrine, thanks to history and the problems of church organization, is ultimately less unacceptable to the Protestant mentality than to the Orthodox. In the final analysis, a Western mind can accept the need for a higher authority that can be called "truly episcopal" for the sake of the well-being of the universal Church, even though refusing to accept what the Roman Catholic Church understands by that term. But for an Orthodox, such a conception of the primacy is theologically intolerable. An immediate and ordinary primatial jurisdiction is literally meaningless, since it contradicts the doctrine of episcopacy.

2. *Papal Infallibility*

Although it is often imperfectly understood, this doctrine perhaps offends Orthodox sensibility less than that of primacy of ordinary and immediate jurisdiction. Some Orthodox still find it difficult to distinguish between "infallibility" and "impeccability". This may seem astonishing to us, but if one analyses the meaning of the term "infallibility" as Vatican I understood it, one has to recognize that the frontiers between the two are not so easy to trace as appears at first sight. The case of a heretical pope is a thorny problem, as is that of the right of a council or of the college of bishops to depose a heretical or publicly scandalous pope. In view of the extremely delicate nature of these questions, it is perhaps not surprising that Chapter III of *Lumen*

Gentium passes them over in silence. Would it have done so if the line dividing infallibility from impeccability had been as clear as we generally suppose it to be?

Whatever the truth of this matter, it remains true that the terms Vatican I chose to define this infallibility; *ex sese, non autem ex consensu Ecclesiae* (DS 3074), appear to the Orthodox as corollaries of the primacy of truly episcopal, immediate and ordinary, jurisdiction. There is certainly some basis for their connection of the two dogmas. So the doctrine of infallibility, applied to the Pontiff as a personal charisma of the bishop of Rome, is another apparently insurmountable obstacle.

II. THE WAY OUT OF THE IMPASSE

Seen in this light, the whole concept of primacy in its specifically Roman Catholic aspects would seem to be totally unacceptable to the Orthodox. Some may regard this as raking in the ashes of the past and point to the hopes of a Vladimar Solovieff. But the picture of Orthodox reactions given here can be substantiated from any Orthodox writings.

So can there be any way out? In human terms, the chances for a dialogue seem slender. Is there any reasonable hope of a council that would be truly ecumenical in Orthodox eyes presenting them with an acceptable image of the Roman primacy? One can be forgiven for doubting it.

Nevertheless, surely there are grounds for thinking that it might be possible to establish and build up a code of practice from which the doctrinal conclusions that logically followed might be drawn? For the Orthodox East, such a practice would be of the greatest importance: concrete gestures count for far more than affirmations of principle in their eyes. I would like now to indicate some lines on which such a practice might be built up, not in an attempt to make the doctrine of Vatican I acceptable, but to progress towards the eventual restoration of sacramental and canonical communion.

(a) We should develop the theology and life of the local Church. Vatican II has established important principles in this field, which are only now beginning to show their implications on the level of the life of the Church. The sacramental life of the local Church is, particularly in the Eucharist, the highest manifestation of the Church in action.

(b) In connection with this, we should stress the necessary relationship, explicitly affirmed by Vatican I (DS 3060), between the *sedens* and the *sedes*, i.e., between the bishop of Rome and his own local Church. This means renouncing a present-day tendency to separate the *sedens* from his *sedes* and put him purely and simply *above* the episcopal college, even though closely related to it. In this respect Vatican II as a whole seems to mark an unfortunate regression in relation to Vatican I, since the See of Rome, the actual basis of the papal primacy, is hardly taken into consideration (with the possible exception of the Decree on Ecumenism, Ch. III, nn. 14 ff., dealing with relations with the Orthodox Churches).

(c) Following the same line, Chapter III of *Lumen Gentium* could have laid more stress on the link between the college of bishops and the local Churches confided to each bishop. This somewhat disincarnate conception of the episcopal college is completely unintelligible in the East, suggesting as it does that this college is above the communion of the local Churches, and even, pushing the concept to its extreme, independent of them. But it is not just bishops, assembled or dispersed, who make up the college, but the bishops as pastors of their respective Churches.

(d) Then, the practical consequences of recognizing local Churches, the principal ones in particular, as sister Churches of the Church of Rome, should be drawn in a more general manner. In order to do this, we need to develop an ecclesiology and a manner of ecclesial life based on communion rather than on power and jurisdiction. Paul VI has already taken courageous steps in this direction, in actions, words and writings that hold considerable promise for the future of relationships with the Orthodox Churches.

(e) This implies taking stock, not only theoretically, but practically and actively, of the fact that the Orthodox Churches have a real autonomy, and a continuous tradition going right back through the Fathers to the apostles. This recommendation is in fact contained in several passages in the Decree on Ecumenism (nn. 14 and 18 in particular). However important the Roman communion may be, the Orthodox Churches have kept their faith and the life of their Churches through all the vicissitudes of their history. This indicates that acceptance of the Vatican I view of papal primacy is not a *sine qua non* condition for possessing this life of faith.

(f) Finally, if we draw the conclusions suggested by these moves, we have to ask ourselves seriously why the complete restoration of canonical and sacramental communion with the Orthodox should not be possible as from now. In other words, at least from the Roman Catholic side, are the reasons for having broken off communion still sufficiently serious to prevent a pure and simple restoration of full communion between the two Churches, pending a later and gradual solution of age-old quarrels? From the Orthodox side, this would mean distinguishing between Rome's affirmations of principles that remain unacceptable, and the actual life of the Roman Church in its present situation. Is such a distinction possible? It certainly cannot be made by requiring Rome to deny what has been defined by earlier councils, but perhaps it might be if the life of the Church in fact carries the day against theoretical principles.

These six points are part of an overall scheme, and cannot be separated from each other. The question at issue is not so much to find out what is acceptable in Catholic teaching on the primacy of the pope and what is not, as to explore together how communion can in fact be regained and lived.

Translated by Paul Burns

Wenzel Lohff

The Papacy and the Reformation
2. *Would the Pope still have been the Antichrist for Luther today?*

IT IS not really possible to give a direct answer to this question, because Luther's polemics against the papacy, which culminated in his equating the pope with the antichrist, had its origin in a very concrete dogmatic controversy about indulgences which ultimately led to a conflict about the foundations of faith itself and of its proclamation.

The whole question was historically conditioned by the situation in which the Church and theology were placed at the time and this situation cannot be adequately reconstructed today by historical interpretation. It was not, in the last resort, determined by biographical considerations. The increasing bitterness with which Luther directed his polemics against the papacy—this is especially noticeable in the text, which he wrote just before his death, against the papacy as "founded by the devil" (*Wider das Papsttum zu Rom, vom Teufel gestiftet 1545*)—can only be understood in the light of the intensification of the struggle between the Roman Church and the churches of the Reformation which were in the process of formation. The whole complex of Church and State politics which formed the background to this controversy is, of course, no longer present in the ecclesiastical situation of today.

I. THE ENEMY IN GOD'S TEMPLE

All the same, the question is still a meaningful one because the dogmatic basis of the question of the proclamation of faith that gave rise to Luther's conflict with Rome has always formed an essential part of Protestant theological teaching and practice. This dogmatic controversy also had an effect on the theology of the Roman Catholic Church. In its simplest form, it presents itself as a question about the unity of the Church in the light of the division of the churches.

For the Roman Catholic Christian, this unity is made present in the office of the pope, but, for the Protestant Christian, this unity has been made uncertain and questionable by Luther's conflict with the papacy. It is, however, not the concrete biographical form of Luther's polemics against the papacy—and especially those in which he engaged during his later years—which needs to be made clearer. What we have to work out in greater detail are the reasons which led to the final breach with Rome and which have continued to make themselves felt in Reformed Christianity up to the present.

Luther's controversy with Rome began as a theological discussion about indulgences, in which Luther insisted that the pope had no right to remit divine punishment for sins and that the right of the pope, as head of the Church, should be restricted to the remission of punishments imposed by the Church alone. In such cases, the essential criterion for Luther was the divine truth of Scripture and the Church's teaching office had, in his opinion, always to be directed towards Scripture and to be subordinate to Scripture. What is more, Scripture had to be interpreted in this case with the essential meaning of the proclamation in mind and this was, according to Luther, the sinner's unconditional acceptance in faith of God's offer of justification. Luther even based his argument about the question of penance and indulgences on this doctrine of justification, regarding himself in this instance not primarily as a reformer, but rather as a theologian of the Church. He was prepared to submit to the judgment of the Roman Curia and believed that the teaching office of the Church was on his side here. He even said that he would tolerate papal condemnation if this were to be pronounced, but he would not regard it as binding on his conscience.

In response to Luther's argument, however, the Church concentrated on the formal question of the plenary powers of the pope. This is clear from the theological opinion of Silvester

Prierias outlined in 1518, from Cardinal Cajetan's demand for submission and above all from Luther's disputation with Eck at Leipzig. Here, an attempt was made to persuade Luther formally to revoke his theological views by using historical evidence of the pope's teaching power.

The only result, however, was that Luther became more and more convinced of the correctness of his own theological position and more and more doubtful of the validity of the historical argument raised against it. He began to re-interpret the Petrine office by a new exegesis of the relevant passages in Scripture (Matthew 4 and John 21) and concluded that the Church's power of the keys could not be thought of as similar to a political power, but that it had rather to be seen as a full power to proclaim the gospel of the grace of Jesus Christ. Peter was the rock of the Church, Luther concluded, because of his faith and his confession: "Thou art the Christ". Christ ruled the Church by his word and his presence was not to be found in the Church as an historical institution, but rather in obedience to his word and to the sacraments instituted by him. Luther did not therefore regard the papacy as outmoded and unnecessary, but simply as lacking any authority which came directly from God. The pope's authority was, he believed, more a sign of and a testimony to this obedience to Christ in history.

He continued to insist, in all his later writings, that he was not contesting the authority of the pope as such, but the abuse of that authority. In all that he wrote during 1520 on the subject of reformation in the Church and especially in his "Epistle to Pope Leo X" and his treatise on Christian freedom (*Von der Freiheit eines Christenmenschen*), both of 1520, he again and again expressed the hope that the Church would acknowledge his claims.

It is true, of course, that, in his reply to Silvester Prierias' *epitome* of 1518, he conditionally expressed the opinion that, if such doctrines were taught in Rome, the "antichrist" must have been ruling there. In using the term "antichrist", a word which was very much in accordance with the apocalyptic ideas prevalent at the time, Luther did not in the first place mean the extreme opponent of the Church, but rather the enemy in God's temple. This was a possibility which he had already discussed in the second lecture on the psalms.

The papal bull, *Exsurge Domine*, of 1520, threatening excommunication, dismissed all doubt in Luther's mind. He called for a general council of the Church and, in reply to the bull, wrote his *Grund und Ursach aller Artikel D. Martin Luthers, so durch römische Bulle unrechtlich verdammt sind 1521.* In this treatise, Luther maintained that the papacy could be considered as a respectable secular power because it suppressed the truth of the gospel, but that the Christian who recognized the pope was denying Christ. This was because the pope had condemned the doctrine of justification, on which man's salvation depended.

From this time onwards, Luther did not deviate from this standpoint. When a general council was eventually convened by Paul III (the Council of Trent), Luther composed in 1537 the Schmalkaldic articles for the League of Protestant Princes and these were later included in the Protestant Confession of Faith. In the case of the papacy, we read, in the 1930 edition of the Confession of Faith of the Lutheran Churches, pp. 427 ff.: "The pope will not allow men to believe (in the sense of the doctrine of justification), but says that, if they obey him, they will be blessed." Luther's conclusion was that the pope, in so doing, set himself above Christ and that men should, for that reason, not obey him.

II. The Papacy in the Sign of Freedom?

The fundamental problem which underlay the conflict between the Reformers and the pope and which ultimately led to a division in the Church may be set out in general terms as follows. The Roman Catholic has confidence in the apostolic authority of the teaching office of his Church which is centralized in the papacy. The Holy Spirit is continuously active throughout history in that office. Orthodox faith and proclamation of that faith is therefore, in the Roman Catholic Church, conditioned by the believer's orientation towards that office as an institution or towards the institutions which have resulted from it in the course of history. This is why the Roman Catholic refutation of Luther's contention was based on historical arguments and a demand to submit to the Church's teaching office. Even Luther and his fellow Protestant theologians based their arguments to a very great extent on *confidence in tradition* and this tradition, though fundamentally scriptural, was also patristic —they made frequent references to the Fathers of the Church.

The concrete conflict which eventually led to the Reformation made Luther question seriously whether the Church's teaching office could always, in every circumstance, guarantee to proclaim faithfully the gospel of Christ. In this sense, then, the Reformation was above all a fundamental *crisis of confidence in the authority of the Church's teaching office*. It was for this reason that a different emphasis was placed, in Protestant teaching, on the meaning and function of the apostolic office. What was stressed above all was that the gospel, as bearing witness to the saving event of Christ, always transcended the institutions of the Church and that all ecclesiastical institutions were there to serve the gospel. There can be no doubt, however, that the authority of the teaching office of the Church is not nowadays regarded in Roman Catholic circles as a purely formal authority with the task of compelling people to accept the teaching proclaimed by the Church. It is abundantly clear from the declaration about religious freedom made by the Second Vatican Council that this authority is always bound to take into account the dignity of the individual human being, who must be left to live in freedom in accordance with his own decision.

What, then, can be said in this context about the doctrine of justification according to the gospel, a question which was, of course, of decisive importance to Luther and the Protestant theologians who followed him? It is clear, both from recent Roman Catholic theological attitudes and from the development that has taken place since the Reformation in the Protestant interpretation of this fundamental doctrine, that the underlying *cause of the original conflict has been almost entirely removed*. In fact, if all the circumstances that I have mentioned are borne in mind, we can almost go so far as to say that the conflict which had its origins in Luther's criticism of the papacy seems now to have been finally settled.

What we still have to bear in mind, however, is that the Reformers' conflict with the papacy had consequences of the utmost importance for the future of Christianity. It led to a new concept of Christian *freedom* and this in turn led to a new interpretation of the institutions of the Church and of the teaching office of the Church in particular. Because it had been rejected by Rome, Protestant teaching was bound to become dependent on confidence in the direct power of the truth of the apostolic gospel. This confidence was further strengthened by scriptural scholarship, which resulted in a certain conviction that the doctrine of justification was unequivocally proclaimed in the Bible. If this is so, then both the institutions and the traditions of the Church have to be examined and verified again and again in the light of Scripture to establish to what extent they serve the gospel and whether they enable the gospel to be proclaimed faithfully or not. They can only be legitimate if they are in accordance with the gospel message.

The institutions and traditions of the Church do, however, come into conflict with the basis of the Church and the unity of the Christian community wherever they become "additional conditions" for receiving salvation (*Confessio Augustana*, art. XVI). From this point of view, the doctrine of justification undoubtedly led to criticism of the Church as a juridical and a teaching institution (*Confessio Augustana*, art. XXI ff.). The Protestant doctrine of justification is therefore basically concerned with the free assurance of salvation through faith and, because this salvation leads to a community, a unity of faith and love, it is both logical and consistent that this community and unity should be visibly present in the outward form of an office. The outcome of Luther's conflict with the papacy and the Protestant understanding of faith that resulted from this controversy, however, meant that this office has again and again to *prove to the believer that it is a true expression of the saving event of Christ.* Unless it can prove its power and authority to express the salvation of Christ, this office cannot demand faith and submission.

In the Protestant sense, faith implies that man is free to ask critically and autonomously about truth, both in so far as it is concerned with the basis of faith and in the sphere of moral decisions. Faith is in danger if decisions made by an authoritative teaching office or sanctions imposed by an institution in the Church stand in the way of this independent assurance of salvation in order to preserve the community of faith. This faith is also equally endangered whenever the individual believer who is subjectively assured of his salvation leaves the community of faith or pursues his own independent course within it and ceases to strive for unity. This, of course, is a problem with which Protestantism has had to struggle throughout its history and which is still acute today.

I said at the beginning of this article that the question "would the pope still have been the antichrist for Luther today?" could not be answered directly. On the basis of the Protestant Christian's experience of the Reformation, the question would now be different. Nowadays, I think, it would be: "Can the office of the papacy be a sign and a testimony today for the Christian believer, enabling him to live in visible unity with the Christian Church and in accordance with the freedom of his faith in the gospel?"

Translated by David Smith

Victor Conzemius

Why was the Primacy of the Pope defined in 1870?

I. A Long Development

"WHEN has definition of doctrine *de fide* been a luxury of devotion and not a stern painful necessity?"[1] Newman's complaint in a letter to (his diocesan) Bishop Ullathorne not only expresses the consternation felt by critically-minded individuals in regard to the elevation as a dogma of the primacy of jurisdiction and infallibility of the Bishop of Rome, but serves as a precise summary definition of the problem facing the Church historian who tries to answer this very question.

In 1870 there was no erroneous doctrine that called in question the essentials of Christian belief. Gallicanism, Jansenism and Josephinism had expired long ago as effective spiritual movements, and no one thought of crusading for a break with Rome. Admittedly there were plenty of problems in regard to the reform of the Church's structure and proclamation, but the Pope made sure that they were of peripheral concern in the Council by deciding that the Fathers should treat the question of his prerogatives before all else. To the historian of theology the Constitution *Pastor Aeternus* of 18 July 1870 is the end explosion of a process of gradual recognition of truth touched off by the Church in its zealous devotion. Of course, from his perspective the Church historian can hardly view the Vatican decrees as a "natural" event, but sees them rather as the culmination of an historical development allowed the final blessing of dogmatic formulation as the result of Roman tactics and proficient stage-managing.

[1] A letter of 28 January 1870, quoted in Wilfrid Ward, *The Life of John Henry Cardinal Newman*, Vol. II (London, 1912), pp. 287–9.

But neither of these two answers satisfies the case and fully explains why the special privileges of the Bishop of Rome were defined *in 1870* without any previous resolution of certain basic ecclesiological problems. The theologian who thinks in abstractions overlooks the fact that the life, piety and development of dogma peculiar to the Church also have quite definite social and societal presuppositions which are major agents of their maturation. On the other hand, the historian who is inclined to ascribe the responsibility for the triumph of "Ultramontanism" to Rome is the willing victim of a sort of Romanism in reverse: he overestimates the power of Rome and forgets that even a clever tactical move on the part of the Pope and the Curia can prevail only when these parties act in accordance with their functional value within the ecclesiastical system. Pope and Curia are also subject to the law of precedent societal, political and social forces that are quite independent of them; only when this is taken into consideration can the historian avoid the danger of positing monocausal explanations.

The definition of the primacy of jurisdiction of the Bishop of Rome put forward by the First Vatican Council is the summit of a more than thousand-year-long development in Roman Catholicism that was not checked but accelerated by the Reformation. The weak and corrupt Papacy of the Reformation period was the only instance that could afford the Tridentine assembly of Catholic forces a regulative centre. Not only the Council but the implementation of the reforms it decreed was to a considerable extent in the Pope's hands. The increase of power and competence that accrued to Rome in exercising its function as unifying centre was directly related to the support sought by bishops and theologians (even in Catholic States) as counterweight to the supreme government in Rome. Certainly not without trouble, yet without paying the price of a schism, Rome succeeded in absorbing those movements which represented a corrective to the trend towards centralization: Gallicanism, which tried with national backing to preserve extensive national autonomy; Episcopalism and Febronianism, which endeavoured from the basis of a theologico-legal consideration of episcopacy to stem the Curial influence; and Josephinism, which—partly out of a consciousness of Christian responsibility—undertook ecclesiastical reforms under State regulation.[2] Hence practice tended to confirm a papalist theory which was able to develop unimpeded thereafter because an effective regulator survived. The societal aspect of the Church, her outward forms of organization and hierarchical elements, were emphasized more strongly than her inward essence. Yves Congar has pointed out that since the sixteenth century the Catholic Church, under the influence of the Jesuits, has subscribed to a definite authoritarian mysticism. This "mysticism" tends to a complete identification of the will of God with the institutional form of authority, in which the voice of God chooses to be heard.[3]

II. DEPENDENCE ON ROME

The French Revolution and the secularization of 1803 provided new and variously contradictory occasions for increased dependence on Rome. Relieved of secular functions, the national Churches in France, Belgium and the German-speaking countries sought closer ties with Rome in order to protect themselves against the interference of State bureaucracies in the ecclesiastical domain. The episcopates of Italy and Spain found the Roman pontiff a natural ally against revolutionary movements engaging in variously aggressive actions against the Church. It was a matter of historical necessity for the young missionary Churches of Canada, North America and Asia (and of course the ascendant Catholic minorities in Britain and Holland) to bind themselves closely to Rome. For the repressed Catholic peoples that had not yet achieved adequate expression of their national aspirations, Rome represented a symbolic hope for better times—even though Irishmen's and Poles' expectations of actual papal support for their legitimate demands were cruelly disappointed.

For its part, the Roman Concordat policy offered the premises of greater freedom from direct State control; the liberal Catholics of France and Italy looked reverently over the Alps to Rome for backing in the implementation of liberal ideas in State and

---

[2] Victor Conzemius, *Katholizismus ohne Rom* (Zürich-Einsiedeln-Cologne, 1969), pp. 15–29.

[3] Yves Congar, "One Historical Development of Authority in the Church", in *Problems of Authority*, ed. J. M. Todd (London, 1964), p. 173.

Church. This is one of the reasons why the liberal Catholics, who unlike the nineteenth-century Papacy had achieved a positive relation with modern freedoms, clung unfailingly to the necessity of the Papal State. Of course they had another motive: they were afraid that a Roman centre relieved of its national-secular concerns would be in a position to increase immeasurably its claim to spiritual sovereignty over the Church.

III. INFALLIBILITY AS A CONDITION OF ORDER

In addition, in the (French) Restoration period an ideological tendency was in evidence which propounded the significance of the Papacy as a moral authority in Church and society. Those who put themselves forward as the standard-bearers of a strong Papacy were mainly laymen: Joseph de Maistre, Lamennais, Donoso Cortes, Louis Veuillot and W. G. Ward (all converts in the broader sense of the term). The Comte de Maistre, who was an opponent of the French Revolution and wrote against it from authoritarian and feudalistic Russia, where he was Sardinian minister to the Court of St Petersburg, "laicized" the question of the papal primacy and infallibility and ensured it an extensive following among the laity; for him the Papacy was the proper centre of the European social order. This *"terrible simplificateur"* was responsible for the following lapidary pronouncement: "No public morality and no national character without religion, no European religion without Christianity, no Christianity without Catholicism, no Catholicism without the Pope, no Pope without the supremacy that is his due." Full and unlimited sovereignty and infallibility were put forward as inalienable prerequisites of State and Church order: "There can be no human society without government, no government without sovereignty, and no sovereignty without infallibility."[4]

Lamennais, de Maistre's fellow countryman and born some thirty years after him, adopted de Maistre's theses in his early

---

[4] See the fundamental essay by Yves Congar, *"L'Ecclésiologie de la Révolution française au concile du Vatican sous le signe de l'affirmation de l'autorité"*, in *Rev. des sciences rel.*, 34 (1960), pp. 77–114; also Victor Conzemius, *Konzil im Bannkreis der Autorität* (Salzburger Forschungs-gespräche, 10) (Salzburg-Munich, 1970).

years of creative activity but smoothed down their harsher features while inserting them in a theological context and drawing the practical conclusions for church life. He made a decisive contribution to the formation of a new Catholic self-consciousness which put the Papacy at the mid-point of its future expectations. Louis Veuillot, editor of the *Univers*, developed and publicized Lamennais's legacy; he strengthened anew the emotional ties between French Catholicism and Rome, to a considerable extent by intentional diminution of episcopal authority.

The English lay theologian W. G. Ward advocated a mechanistic conception of authority—even to the extent of remarking that he would gladly have a new encyclical or authoritative interpretation from the Pope with his breakfast each morning. The Spanish philosopher of culture Donoso Cortes was in the line of French traditionalism; for him genuine authority could come only from without and must be ratified from without.

IV. The Cult of the Papacy and the Threat to the Church States

In the second half of the nineteenth century this publicists' crusade on behalf of the Papacy (gladly accepted but in no way stage-managed by Rome) led to the formation of a neo-Ultramontane bloc held together by an ideologically rigid papal cult varying from extravagant declarations of loyalty to the Pope to blasphemous and squalid virtual identifications of the Pope with Christ. A few weeks before his death the ardent Romanist Montalembert spoke out vehemently against the advocates of absolutism in the Church who had set up their idol in the Vatican.[5] It was very significant that this papal mysticism was not confined to small, esoteric circles but infected the laity in general and mobilized them on the side of the Papacy. A strengthening of papal authority was in accordance with the wishes and ideas of the Catholic "basis".

The catalyst for this hitherto unknown increase in pro-papal sympathies among the laity was provided by the question of the States of the Church. Despite the support provided by French

[5] Roger Aubert, *Le pontificat de Pie IX (1846–1878)* (Paris, 1952), p. 345.

troops for the worldly sovereignty of the Pope, the days of this ecclesiastical paradigm of the State were numbered. It was only a question of how long the Pope, abandoned by the Powers, would be suffered to remain as ruler of the increasingly reduced Papal States. In this situation the Pope succeeded in assembling the faithful on his side. What Lamennais had proposed as the most pressing task of the Church of the future—the alliance of the Papacy and the people—now came about, but in the opposite direction to that envisaged by Lamennais. The Pope was not to place himself at the head of the emancipation process, but to take advantage of the moral pressure of the Catholic masses in order to extend his position.

Admittedly the personal charm of Pius IX, his quick-wittedness and unforced popular manner, had much to do with this development. Yet the Pope would hardly have been well received by the masses had they not spontaneously identified themselves with his cause: the common people found in the suffering Pope abandoned by the politicians an appropriate object upon which to focus their sense of fairness and justice—something for which the effort seemed worth while. The donation of "Peter's Pence" was once again imposed; and among those who declared themselves ready to defend with body and soul the Pope's life and the continuance of the Papal States, the Dutch were particularly prominent. Not merely attachment to the Holy Father but concern for the future existence of the Church called for an increase in papal authority for the Church's sake.

V. The Growth of the Ghetto Mentality

One would be mistaken in concluding that the preservation of the States of the Church was the sole effective consideration behind the summoning of the Council. It was certainly a contributory suasion, but politically inclined Cardinals such as Secretary of State Antonelli did not look favourably upon the plan for a Council, since they feared that new difficulties for the States would arise from the draft decrees of the extreme papalist wing. Yet the mentality indicated here is significant: the atmosphere before the Council was characterized by a defensive attitude all along the line: rejection of the revolutionary movements, of political liberalism, of contemporary philosophical trends, of Bible criticism, of Protestantism—in short, the erection of barricades against an inimical world. Essentially, it was not the attitude to the Papacy but the attitude to the world that was to split the bishops into two factions at the Council.[6]

How far there was any real chance historically of correcting this kind of reaction and of preventing the subsequent growth of a ghetto mentality remains an open question for researchers. Pius IX and his Jesuit advisers saw no other solution than the compensation of a dwindling ecclesiastical influence in State and society by retreating to the Church's own territory and strengthening the power of the Roman executive. After the failure of his liberal politics and his return from exile in Gaeta, Pius IX settled for this religious direction. Hence the promulgation as dogma in 1854 of the Immaculate Conception of Mary was simultaneously an expression of adulation for Pius in person and of the new flowering of adulation for Mary; but it was just as much a manifestation of his high office and a protest against the spirit of the age.

Behind this apparently devotional dogma there was a quite specific understanding of the Church: not only its content but the form of its promulgation was important in the eyes of Rome. Although the Pope did consult the bishops of the world beforehand, he made the act of proclamation an *ex cathedra* decision, thus anticipating the prerogatives accorded him at the First Vatican Council.[7] The *Civiltà Cattolica* clearly emphasized the dogma as proceeding from the Pope's teaching office, and the Jesuit Schrader, Professor of Dogmatics at the Collegium Romanum from 1852 to 1857, was able to write thus in 1864: "Pius IX did not offer a theological definition of papal infallibility on December 8th 1854, but laid practical claim to it."[8] There is no need to

---

[6] Victor Conzemius, "Die Minorität auf dem Ersten Vatikanischem Konzil", in Theologie u. Phil., 45 (1970), pp. 409–34.

[7] See S. Gruber, Mariologie u. kath. Selbstbewusstsein (Beiträge zur Neueren Gesch. d. kath. Theol., 12) (Essen, 1970); Roger Aubert, "L'Episcopat belge et la proclamation du dogme de l'Immaculée Conception en 1854", in Ephem. Theol. Lov., 31 (1955), pp. 63–99; G. Müller, "Die Immaculata Conceptio im Urteil der mitteleuropäischen Bischöfe", in Kerygma u. Dogma, 14 (1968), pp. 46–68; G. Müller, "Theolog. Erkenntnis u. päpstl. Infallibilität", in Festschrift für W. v. Loewenich (Witten, 1968), pp. 182–92. [8] C. Schrader, Pius IX als Papst u. als König, III (1865), p. 12.

stress the fact that the 1864 Syllabus with its undifferentiated condemnation of modern freedoms was a test-case for the emphasizing of the papal teaching office. From mid-century there was an increase in the initiatives to impose recognitions of the papal primacy and infallibility on provincial synods. The bishops who assembled in Rome in 1867 to commemorate the death of the leading apostles Peter and Paul were required to attest to the papal prerogatives in the terms of the (in any case generally accepted) formulation of the Council of Florence.

And yet one would have to ignore historical reality in order to view the Council as a convention of obedient bishops neatly manipulated by Rome. Most of the bishops did not need to be brought round to the Roman estimate of the situation. They already thought of themselves in categories which tended to a strengthening of authority.[9] For not only the dogmatic papal teachings but the Constitution on Christian Faith heavily emphasizes authority.[10] It is necessary to study the bishops' mentality more rigorously than has been customary in order to understand the implication that they thought their standpoint would have for the life of the Church.[11] In the spiritual crisis of the time, in contradistinction to the philosophical systems which were ranged against Christianity and offered a substitute for religion, and not least of all in view of the hardly hopeful prospects before the ecclesiastical centre in Rome, a strengthening of this very centre seemed necessary and inevitable. During the debate on the papal primacy the following dictum went the rounds in Rome: The theologians (among the bishops) are against it; the practical men and the missionaries are for it. This is possibly a simplification; nevertheless this observation shows that the issue was pre-decided in the area of piety and practical church affairs at least.

For Pius IX, who was in no way a cool and calculating enlarger of his personal power and majesty, but an easily excitable

[9] J. D. Acton, "The Vatican Council", in History of Freedom and other Essays (London, 1907), pp. 492 ff.

[10] H. J. Pottmeyer, Der Glaube vor dem Anspruch der Wissenschaft (Freiburg-Basle-Vienna, 1969).

[11] Cf. my article (n. 6 above), and Roger Aubert, "Motivations théologiques et extra-théologiques des partisans et des adversaires de la définition dogm. de l'infaillibilité du pape à Vatican I", in L'Infaillibilité. Son aspect philos. et théol., ed. E. Castelli (Paris, 1970), pp. 91–103.

man who pressed ahead in answer to the appropriate contradictory stimulus from without, devotion was the motive determining the readiness with which he accelerated plans for the dogmatic establishment of the papal primacy and infallibility. The elevated conception he had of his office and the impetus he hoped the life of the Church would receive enabled him to see beyond the considerations of the Curial (!) Presidents of the Council, to remove the section on the Roman pontiff from the schema *De Ecclesia*, and to ensure it priority treatment in the second half of the Council.[12]

These preconditions made it possible to define the papal prerogatives at the First Vatican Council. The concept of "devotion" which Newman used to characterize the spiritual impetus of definition as a "luxury" cannot be rejected out of hand but requires further qualification. Fear and apprehension, opportunism and pragmatism, and paradigms of society drawn from the ecclesiastical Middle Ages are contributory factors. That explanations on the basis of the *theological* presuppositions for this kind of definition fall short of the whole truth is a finding from which the theologian must draw certain conclusions.[13] In addition, it should lead theologians to see more clearly that Councils (Vatican II as well) are dependent on the social presuppositions of their time. This insight would allow the theologian who remains steadily attuned to the gospels a measure of critical enlightenment in regard to his own traditions but also in regard to the spirit of the age; a not unwelcome by-product of this attitude would be an increase of modesty and soberness in view of his heavy dependence on the world that lies about him.

[12] M. Maccarone, *Il Concilio Vaticano I e il Giornale di Mons. Arrigoni* (Italia Sacra, 7) (Padua, 1966), pp. 334 ff.
[13] Hans Küng, *Unfehlbar? Eine Anfrage* (Zürich-Einsiedeln-Cologne, 1970).

Translated by John Griffiths

Alexandre Ganoczy

How can one evaluate Collegiality vis-à-vis Papal Primacy?

VATICAN II was "Collegiality as lived". The manner and main object of its thought met in the same line of research. In our post-conciliar situation things are not the same. The doctrine of Collegiality runs up against problems of application and development. Hence we have to question ourselves as to the way it has been implemented in the two domains of theory and practice. The progress of ecumenical convergence between the Churches depends on the outcome of this new questioning. We hope to contribute to the debate by making certain principles more explicit and by putting forward various practical suggestions.

I. THEORETICAL PRINCIPLES

(a) The "Communional" Principle

One of the predominant tendencies of contemporary ecclesiology consists in situating particular structures within *all-embracing structures*. Inspired by the hermeneutical principle according to which that which is a part—even an eminent part—cannot be properly understood or interpreted save by the mediation of the total reality, the exponents of this tendency have acquired the habit of approaching the particular priesthood from the standpoint of the universal priesthood, the special ministries from the standpoint of "general ministeriality", the Council from the standpoint of "fundamental conciliarity" and episcopal Collegiality from the standpoint of the *all-embracing communion* of the people of God. It was in this sense, it seems, that Paul VI spoke at the 1969 Synod of a "progress of the ecclesial communion towards the summit which is episcopal Collegiality".

The term "communion" is used with many shades of meaning ranging from the mystical to the juridical. In a general way, however, it is used to describe the theological content of the two biblical names for the Christian community, namely the Body of Christ and the People of God. Hence the word "communion" evokes a community of people who, as regards essentials, possess no supremacy over each other but are united in a *common submission* of faith to Christ or God to whom alone belongs this "Body" or this "People". All are equally *servi Dei* or *servi Christi*.

We must note that this idea tends in fact to transform even the classical conception of the "hierarchy". When one speaks, for instance, of "hierarchical communion" the accent is no longer on the vertical classification of ministers and hence believers, but on their free and brotherly *organic co-ordination*. In other words the *cum* wins over the *sub*. The image of a separated summit gives way to that of an integrated centre. And the order of life little by little takes over priority from the order of law (necessary in other contexts).

It is true that concerning the totality of these points, language trails behind the reality envisaged. The communional formulas still preserve much of their typically ancient meaning. The Pauline image of the body, applicable to the local community, is a Christian variant of the Greco-Roman image of the city (and as such original). As for the theme of the body dominated and determined by a "transcendent" head which the Ephesians and the Colossians applied to the universal Church, it was borrowed in part from a Gnostic image of the cosmos. In both cases we must note the influence of the speculations of subsequent Judaism on Adam, the original and universal man who carries within him the destiny of all his descendants.

If we consider the complex image currently given of our societies by the sociological and political sciences, we cannot avoid noticing a time-lag between the ancient description and the contemporary reality of the Church. While the former suggests an *ineluctable* solidarity organically determined, harmonizing with an ethic of communication, the latter is seen to be conditioned by the ideal of a community that forms itself *freely*, of which the relationships are scientifically modifiable and which is animated by an ethic of *conflict* necessary to progress.

We could make an analogous comment concerning the image of "the people of God". The *laos tou theou* has a typically ancient character. It is the *theocratic* community, the flock that docilely follows its king-shepherd, its God who gives it everything through providence and the ministers chosen by him. The contemporary reality of the Church on the other hand is marked by a *democratic* environment, or one on its way to democratization.

What direction does post-conciliar research take with regard to all this? It upholds biblical conceptuality but interprets and translates it into a modern idiom. Thus it was that Paul VI was able to speak at the recent Synod of the "solidary *co-responsibility*" of the episcopal college in the context of the "mystical body". This formula, which also points to collaboration between priests and laity, obviously derives from the vocabulary of modern democracy. We cannot trace it back to *laos tou theou* and still less to *sooma tou Christou*. To find its derivation in antiquity we would have to look to the political notion of *demos* and the politico-religious notion of *ekklesia*. *Demos* signifies a general mass of citizens gathered together for a specific end, informed or even convinced as to the benefits of this end and invited to "organize of itself"—through adequate representative organs— the public affairs corresponding to it. Already we have a sort of prefiguration of our co-responsible communities. So it is not without reason that "democracy" possesses in *"demos"* its etymological root. As for the term *ekklesia*, it contains the dynamic idea of *convocation* produced with a view to making *free* and aware subjects participate in political and cultural union. Here, too, there is the beginning of modern co-responsibility.

It remains a well-known fact, however, that the government of the Church will never be able to be modelled on democatic political regimes—though certain elements of these have their obvious place in contemporary ecclesial structures. So its own specific originality must be safeguarded when the element of "co-responsibility" is introduced into it. It is in its own *sui generis* way that the people of God must take to itself what the world has to offer it.

To sum up: the "communional" principle appears at the point of junction between the Christian community and its governmental structures. The idea underlying it epitomizes the content of the biblical names for the Church which refer above all to *divine domination*. But it nevertheless remains capable of integrating anthropological elements and modern political ones which put more emphasis on *human freedom*. Understood in this way, the ecclesial communion can and should be the all-embracing reality on which episcopal Collegiality naturally draws.

(b) *The Principle of Representation*

The formula "people of God" is often used in an ill-defined way. Now the safeguard of ecclesial identity, introduced when necessary historical changes are made, demands that the use of this formula should show forth both its original meaning and the meaning it takes on in our contemporary conditions of existence. Otherwise there is a risk of, for example, projecting a socializing present on to a theocratic past, or of making desperate attempts to restore a Christendom with sacral structures in a secularized age.

When we seek to situate Collegiality within the all-embracing reality of "the people of God", it is essential that we should respect this irreversible relationship of the past with the present. And we must respect it in such a way that from the past there may emerge all that is priceless in the original and definitive revelation, while in the present there may appear the contemporary form (*Gestalt*) that the original and definitive revelation must assume to ensure it is still perceived as such. Here lies the most elementary requirement of the *eschatological historicity* of the Church. It must be shown that the people of God, because it is of God, is constructed with ministries raised up and ordained by God, but also that this people, because it is a human community of today, forms and exercises these ministries according to the requirements of mankind today. In taking on a ministry a given believer becomes *a representative of Christ* in a special way, but he must become it along strictly contemporary lines so that he will also be *a representative of the community*.

And what are these contemporary lines if not those which best

88   ALEXANDRE GANOCZY

interpret the freely expressed choice of co-responsible people? If someone objects that in the Church the sovereignty of God can never be replaced by the sovereignty of the people, our answer is that we are not suggesting such a replacement; we are discussing the idea of taking seriously in a modern context Our Lord's desire to *identify himself* with all the members of his kingdom, starting with "the littlest ones". And supposing it pleases him in our day to exercise his inalienable sovereignty through the *mediation* of the ministerial "sovereignty" of his *demos* or his *ekklesia*—who are we to reproach him?

Here we could indicate as a line of research what I would call an *encounter* between christological representation and popular-ecclesial representation. On the one hand each member of the faithful (Matt. 25. 31–46), each "basic group" (Matt. 18. 20), each particular church represents Christ and makes him validly present; because it is his Spirit that unites them. On the other hand the same people or groups or communities are structured in such a way that more restricted groups represent larger groups. Thus such-and-such a portion of mankind having such-and-such a culture finds its representation in a particular Church which lives within it and for it. In this Church such-and-such a sector calls in its turn for such-and-such lay and priestly representatives. The totality of the sectors thus tends to give itself such-and-such synodal representation.

Finally all this movement becomes still more concentrated at the episcopal level where universal representation is produced thanks to the College united round the Pope. It is evident that only Christ is sovereignly represented, by means of sacramental and charismatic graces. His people, even if it carries this sovereignty ministerially, can do no more than make its laborious way through the maze of the techniques of representation. The application of these techniques, among which first place goes to *democratic election*, of course does not proceed without risks: manipulation, partisan rivalries, dictatorship of the majority over minorities, the elected turning tyrannically against his electors. But these risks are reduced to reasonable proportions if appropriate methods are employed. And "appropriate" means "contemporary": it is illusory to expect medieval methods to cope with the difficulties of the universal suffrage of our time.

(c) *The Principle of Reciprocity*

This principle is revealed by the famous *"quoque"* of *Lumen Gentium*, 22: the Pope possesses "full, supreme and universal power" over the Church, but the order of bishops, in union with the Pope, is *also* the subject of "supreme and full power over the universal Church". What does this *"quoque"* mean? Does it mean that there are *two* subjects of supreme ministerial power— one that could be called "capital" and the other that could be called "corporative"? If so, must we understand the relations between the two in the following way: the second, the one representing collectively the universal Church, ceases to exist as such if it is not united to the first, while the first, as representative of Christ as his vicar, never ceases to be this, even if he "frees himself" at will (*ad placitum!*) from the second?

Such an interpretation of Collegiality can certainly be put forward from numbers 3 and 4 of the *Nota praevia*. But equally it can be ruled out on the basis of declarations such as that of the "Seper Report" to the 1969 Synod. This specifies that the primatial ministry is subject (*subicitur*) not only to the word of God but also to the "original constitution of the Church". Now this constitution is essentially "communional" and thus understands Collegiality as a fundamental law of the ministry. So Collegiality binds in a qualitatively identical way, though according to diverse moralities, Peter and his "successors" just as much as the other apostles and their "successors".

It follows that it is not at all easy to apply the old analogy of body and head to the relationship "episcopacy-primacy". And the difficulty becomes insurmountable in proportion as the Christo-ecclesiological vision of Colossians and Ephesians is taken as model. For how would we dare to compare the "plenitude" of Christ in relation to his Church with the "plenitude" of the purely ministerial power of the Pope in relation to the power of the episcopal body (equally "plenary" in any case)? No defender of the title "Vicar of Christ" would be so foolhardy as to go as far as that. But if this is how things are, why insist so much on the postulate that the body of bishops can do nothing, at the "supreme" and universal level, without its *"caput"*, whereas the *"caput"* can in principle do everything, "at all times", "freely" and *"seorsum"*, without the body of bishops?

If we stand by the old metaphor, would it not be better to suggest the following: just as a body without a head can neither live nor act, similarly (*pari modo!*) a head without a body cannot do so either? To follow this line of argument is to open the way to a certain *principle of reciprocity*—which could lead to completely levelling out the primacy and thus be incompatible with the dogma of Vatican I and II. However, this danger exists only if we adopt the hypothesis of an absolutely *symmetrical* and egalitarian reciprocity, and disappears in the hypothesis of a *functionally differentiated* reciprocity.

It will then be possible to maintain constructively that the Pope and the bishops *cannot* exercise their respective functions one *against* the other, and should not whatever the circumstances do so one *without* the other. Certainly the Pope will fulfil his functions as necessary and irreplaceable *leader* of the College, and the bishops will fulfil their functions as necessary and irreplaceable directing *members* of the same College. It is here that lies their specific functional difference whose historically legitimate basis is the Petrine-apostolic model. But that does not in any way prevent the application of a wider "policy of dialogue" between the two conjoined subjects or, if one prefers, between the two ministries constituting the single collegial subject of "supreme" power.

(d) *The Principle of Co-ordination*

The theology of particular Churches is today in full development. Without it the representation of bishops on the universal plane would not have sufficient weight to permit it to found a true reciprocal dialogue with the Pope. Moreover, this theology is the basis of what is called *horizontal Collegiality*.

What is this about? It is about a strictly ecclesiological explication of the differences and divergences inherent in the historically, geographically and sociologically universal and Catholic existence of the people of God. As each particular Church represents the portion of mankind from which it springs, all are called upon to communicate to each other, as it were, the "riches of the nations". It is not by mutually "exporting" or "importing" their respective patrimonies that they respond to this call, but valid communication is made *first* at the level of mutual understanding: a condition *sine qua non* of all effective co-operation.

Let us put it more concretely. It is natural that the understanding of the being and doing of the Church should be conditioned in, for instance, prosperous Germanic communities—enjoying a concordatory regime and benefiting from a long philosophical tradition—quite otherwise than in African communities in the process of economic development, living perhaps under a dictatorial regime and have traditions enriched by the contributions of animism and tribalism. Now catholicity demands that these various ways of understanding should be able to subsist in their historical diversity, should be able to found different ecclesiologies and *thus* become the basis for those multiple dialogues that concretize the innate unity of the Church.

That the self-understanding of each community should become the object of mutual understanding: that is the basic task to be accomplished. Its achievement requires first and foremost that those locally, regionally and continentally responsible should put themselves constantly in a state of convergence, for they are aware more than anyone else of the diversities proper to each aggregate. But it is common knowledge that these diversities, even after having been taken over and co-ordinated by those responsible, can transform themselves into divergences, antagonisms and destructive confrontations.

It is then that a *centre of harmony and world co-ordination* is proved to be not only useful but indispensable. As soon as Catholic convergence finds itself threatened, the arbitration and moderation of a well-informed centre "geared" to that end will be able to restore it. The judgments of this court of appeal will be doctrinal, ethical or jurisdictional in character. They will never be arbitrary inasmuch as they will follow the Spirit of Christ which blows where it wills, and the court will agree to being conditioned by the situation of the parties having recourse to it. To affirm that the charism of "Petrine" primacy is accorded to the Pope with a view to this function of co-ordination is to evaluate it in terms of the actual needs of his ministry—a ministry then seen as the guarantee of ecclesial communion and, hence, of episcopal Collegiality.

One often hears talk in this context of the principle of *subsidiarity*. This signifies, *grosso modo*, that the primatial function leaves the episcopal ministry to act in full freedom so long as it is straightforwardly exercising the powers that fall within its competence in the government of a particular Church. The Pope reserves certain rights to himself, and intervenes directly, only in cases where safeguarding the unity of faith and communion demands it. Those who profit by subsidiarity obviously run the risk of falling into excessive particularism, but this risk can be reduced by putting into practice the principle of *solidarity*: i.e., no community will use its freedom *to the detriment* of any other community. This requirement is sometimes extremely painful for those who advance along the path of reform and progress more rapidly than others. But true ecclesial co-ordination is achieved only at this price: no subsidiarity without solidarity.

II. Some Practical Suggestions

(a) For a "Communional" Law

The reform of canon law is under way, but is it guided by strictly contemporary ecclesiological and juridical principles? Tertullian and Cyprian, both jurists and theologians, knew how to initiate a system within which the ecclesial reality *of their time* was expressed in the terms of Roman public law. It was thus that they conferred a juridical meaning on the notion of *communio* which harmonized well with the strictly sacramental and ecclesial *koinoonia*. Today we live under the aegis of pluralism, secularization and democratization. Besides which, communion is seen as a reality bringing together Churches in a state of *mission*. Thus the new "Code" must borrow widely from modern international and public law while expressing the missionary condition of this "brotherhood of Churches" that the universal Church is tending to become. Constituting as it does the juridical superstructure, relative but indispensable to the communional infrastructure of the people of God, this "Code" should *therefore* define Collegiality and its modalities in performance.

(b) For Representative "Colleges" at every level

Sacramental consecration makes a bishop a representative of

Christ. "Canonical determination" confers on him the possibility of fulfilling his functions in accordance with the demands of co-ordination. But it is to be hoped that bishops may become more representative of their communities and that therefore the authority of the episcopal College may increase. To this end, modern variants of the ancient *discipline of election* should be worked out. Hippolytus's "apostolic tradition", which entrusts the choice of bishops to the people and the presbyterium, could serve— *mutatis mutandis*—as model.

At the Synod of 1969 it was suggested that the co-responsible action of the Church should henceforth be taken over by *assemblies of elected people* in every homogeneous sector. The Belgian Priests' Councils have asked that "working groups" should be set up, "representative of all the people of God"—lay councils, pastoral councils, councils of experts, "spokesmen of diverse tendencies"—the whole (by the intermediary of the bishops and at their side) converging on the world Synod and its permanent Secretariat. Cardinal Suenens, for his part, has asked whether the Synod could not be associated with the College of Cardinals in electing the Pope. . . .

However this may be, there is reason to point out that a more generalized electoral procedure would allow for the deployment of the charisms freely bestowed among various members of the communities by the Spirit—so that a charismatic co-responsibility could play the role devolving on it in the guiding of the universal Church.

(c) *For Synodal Deliberative Powers*

No corporative action of the body without the head, no capital action of the head without the body. This ideal of reciprocity will never be truly achieved so long as the world Synod remains a purely consultative organism and not a deliberative one.

In the first case the Pope alone proposes and disposes. With the help of his Curia it is he who decides the form and content of the schema about which he will consult the Synod as and when he thinks it opportune. The Synod then acts along the lines of a "Pontifical Commission" whose majority advice (cf. *Humanae Vitae!*) can be equally well accepted or rejected by the Pope. But with a deliberative voice the Synod will be able to play a different part; it will be able to contribute to the proposal of matters to be discussed, it will formulate them in all freedom, and even ask for the convocation of a session if the majority of its members thinks it necessary. The preliminary deliberations will also in large measure be a task falling within the competence of "horizontal Collegiality". During the session itself the Pope and the assembly will deliberate *together*—no more keeping silence "out of discretion"!—even if the right of final approval still lies with the Pope. Inasmuch as these debates conform to the principle of "functionally differentiated" reciprocity, inevitable confrontations will have more chance of ending up in reasonable compromise rather than in disastrous breakdown. There, too, primatial authority risks nothing in letting itself become more "dialogal".

(d) For "Informal Meetings" between Members of the College

This proposal was made at the last Synod. It corresponds to common practice in modern political life while conforming to the "communional" nature of the people of God. What the heavy machinery—half-curial, half-academic—of the numerous general assemblies cannot give often springs spontaneously from these "intercommunions of charity" which are the encounters of person with person. In many cases it is during a friendly meal that diverse aspirations, interests and opinions are best co-ordinated. And why should the Pope and the bishops not multiply their personal contacts with responsible Christian groups while cutting down on their solemn appearances before crowds that are enthusiastic, yes, but incapable of co-responsibility?

Would not such contacts favour the translation into action of the great principles of communion, co-responsibility, representation and reciprocity—all of which open the way to raising the value of Collegiality at all levels?

Translated by Barbara Wall

John E. Lynch

Advantages and Drawbacks of a Centre of Communications in the Church

1. *Historical Point of View*

I. How were Communications Practised?

FROM the very beginning the various local Christian communities were acutely conscious of the intimate relationship that bound them one with another. The liturgical practice of several bishops participating in an episcopal consecration emphasized that an individual bishop possessed his episcopacy only in communion with other bishops. Christians who moved from one area to another carried letters of communion which ensured them of fraternal welcome. Every large church, especially one in a metropolis, kept a list of the principal churches of the world with which it was in communion. Recognition or acceptance by the oldest or apostolic churches was of great importance. In the case of the Roman Church such recognition was crucial, for, according to St Ambrose, "from it there spreads to all the other churches the rights of communion that must be honoured" (Ep. 11, 4; PL 16:946).

To be in communion meant above all to share the same faith and to participate in the same sacramental life of the Eucharist. As new problems arose it was imperative for the various churches to exchange information so that the response to changing circumstances would not be radically different and communion thereby destroyed. Reports of synodal decisions were accordingly transmitted to Rome and to other Christian communities.

When questions of central importance and great urgency arose, such as concerned christology, written reports would not suffice, but it would be necessary to convene an ecumenical assembly.

During the first eight centuries it was the Emperor who proved to be the "communications centre"; he considered it his God-given responsibility to summon such a council and to guide it to a conclusion. By dialogue and personal communication many disputes were seen to stem, in part at least, from a difference in terminology. The conciliar enactments marking off areas of heresy fulfilled the biblical function of witness in as much as agreement on vital issues was seen as a sign of the Spirit. All the major Christian Churches, Orthodox, Lutheran, Anglican and Reformed join in reverencing the first four ecumenical councils, recognizing in them "the pure and genuine exposition of Scripture, which the holy fathers applied with spiritual prudence to crush the enemies of religion who had then arisen (Calvin, *Institutes*, IV, 9, 8).[1]

In addition to providing a test or check of orthodoxy, a centre of communications offers a safeguard against local vindictiveness and arbitrary action. In the glare of publicity petty and unreasonable action so opposed to the Christian spirit will be unmasked to the shame of the offenders. The Council of Nicaea in c. 5, the first official regulation dealing with episcopal synods, required the bishops of a province to assemble twice a year for the main purpose of reviewing excommunications pronounced within the province. The examination was to prevent any abuse occasioned by "narrowness of mind, by pertinacity, or any other vice of a bishop".

More than against a despotic bishop, the Church needed protection from the tyranny of a feudal lord. During the Merovingian period when communications with the papacy were badly disrupted, ecclesiastical affairs and morals generally fell to a low ebb. The strong hand of Charlemagne brought about a temporary restoration only to be followed by worse evils. The Gregorian Reform with its programme of councils, papal legates and monastic exemptions offered a more enduring escape from the strangulation of local rapacity. When the papacy finally allied itself with the reform spirit of Cluny, Christian ideals could once

[1] For the attitude of various Christian churches see *The Councils of the Church, History and Analysis*, ed. H. J. Margull, Philadelphia, 1966. (*Die ökumenischen Konzile der Christenheit*, Evangelisches Verlagswerk, Stuttgart, 1961.)

more transcend territorial barriers to exert a quickening effect throughout Western Christendom.

The primary service of a communications centre is to *promote* high standards of liturgy, discipline, in a word, *ecclesiastical style*. From its very birth the Church was organized along the political and geographical lines of the Roman Empire. It was quite natural for the churches in a given province to look to the church in the political capital for leadership. Churches in the largest cities such as Alexandria, Antioch and Rome gradually gained an ascendancy in their respective areas of influence. Just as these centres set the fashion in culture so would they become models in ecclesiastical matters. Since the New Testament deals with ultimate moral principles rather than with concrete and specific problems (Luke 12. 13–16), Christian communities were left on their own to work out regulations specifying rights and duties. In time the trend towards uniformity within an area would lead to the institution of the *patriarchates*. The practice gradually developed for individual churches for the sake of better administration and a more aesthetic worship to cede some of their independence to the patriarch. The origin of this institution was, then, a concession from below rather than an imposition from above. The Council of Nicaea which canonized this development (c. 6) speaks of it as an ancient custom by A.D. 325. In matters of discipline and liturgy this arrangement had the advantage of providing for regional difference and avoiding fragmentary isolation.

In the West, *Rome*, the only apostolic see, was virtually without competition. Due to its "greater headship" (Peter and Paul) as well as to its position as the ancient capital of the Empire, the Church of Rome was looked to for ecclesiastical leadership and guidance. Letters came to the Eternal City from all over the Christian world posing questions, seeking advice and requesting norms. In answer to these appeals there arose the papal decretals towards the end of the fourth century. It was natural, too, that when the papacy sent out missionaries to evangelize certain areas that correspondence would be exchanged settling problems encountered. Rome once more assumed a position of leadership under Leo IX 1049–1054) and his successors, especially Gregory VII (1073–1085). From this renewed centre a programme of reform and higher standards was communicated to the rest of Western Christendom. The specific goals of the renewal were transmitted chiefly through the new canon law collections of the period.

An important agency of reform communication was also the papal legate. Gregory VII used legates with great effectiveness, sending them to Denmark, Norway, Sweden, Poland, Hungary and Spain. He assigned them a wide assortment of charges, but above all they were to work through local synods in spreading the work of reform. Henceforth the legates became an indispensable organ for papal communication throughout Christendom.

II. DISADVANTAGES

In the following centuries the papacy became too preoccupied with political affairs. The failure of the fifteenth-century councils to undertake any serious reform programme made the Protestant Reformation inevitable. Then after a series of disasters and the protracted sessions of Trent, it was left to the papacy to devise rigid standards for holding the line against further erosion. The papacy communicated to the Catholic world in minutest detail what publications were harmful ("The Index", 1564), what doctrine was to be preached (the "Catechism"), what liturgy was to be observed (Breviary and Missal). A Church under siege had to be uniform in every respect and intolerant of any deviation.

The disadvantages of a communication centre are obvious. Uniformity tends to become a value out of all proportion to the general well-being of the Church. Initiative is stifled. Programmes and practices easily become stereotyped. Old forms are reluctantly discarded even when the circumstances that gave rise to them no longer exist. Solutions that worked in the past are too readily assumed to be valid for the present. Authority gives the impression of being the guardian of decrepit and dead forms.

The mission history of the Church bears painful testimony to the harm wrought by rigid uniformity. The work of SS. Cyril and Methodius failed in Moravia and Pannonia due in part to their use of the Slavic liturgy. According to prevalent Western opinion God should be praised only in Hebrew, Greek and Latin in accord with the trilingual tablet on the Saviour's cross (P.L.

83:182C; MGH, Ep. VI, 459). Again the remarkably successful work inaugurated by the Jesuit Matteo Ricci in Peking about 1600 was abruptly brought to a halt a century later in 1704 when Pope Clement XI absolutely forbade the Chinese rites. The majority of the native clergy apostatized and the emperor expelled all missionaries for this affront to native customs.

Another ill-effect of a communications centre is that it encourages an abdication of local responsibility and too readily leads to polarization and an escalation of tension. A classic case is that of Martin Luther.[2] In 1517 Luther, a professor at Wittenburg, wrote to his Archbishop Albrecht about the scandal caused by Tetzel's inaccurate theology of indulgences. This appeal was couched in respectful tones, confident that ecclesiastical authority would take proper action. The issue raised was theological and logical, not particularly profound, dealing with the practical order. The Archbishop did not offer Luther the courtesy of a reply but promptly denounced him to Rome. The Archbishop abnegated his responsibility by forwarding the matter to a curia only too willing to take charge. The theological context was soon forgotten and a judicial process begun culminating in Luther's excommunication. Had the case been referred to a local theological commission or to the North German bishops meeting in Halle in November 1517, who can say what would have happened! How many other cases could have been settled more amicably and efficiently closer to the point of origin where all the circumstances were known. Would Pius V have excommunicated Queen Elizabeth in 1570 if he realized he was placing English Catholics in the position of traitors? Some situations are too complicated to be adequately understood in a distant centre. Even the papal legates sent to Constantinople in 861 to investigate the deposition of the Patriarch Ignatius concurred with the decision in favour of Photius, despite the fact that Pope Nicholas had reserved judgment to himself (MGH, Ep. VI, 514).

Throughout Christian history there has been tension between liberty and conformity, variety and uniformity. Some centre of communication is necessary to counteract the fissiparous tendencies of *sola scriptura* which has a logical culmination in the

---

[2] R. E. McNally, "The Roman Process of Martin Luther", in *Canon Law Society of America Symposium*, 1969.

autonomous congregation which recognizes no church beyond its walls. At the other extreme few would be anxious to return to the pre-Vatican II state of the Roman Catholic liturgy where every gesture of the priest at Mass was prescribed down to the positioning of the fingers. Recourse to a centre of communication need not, as in the past, lead to an elimination of desirable variety but rather make the richness of the Christian experience accessible to all. It is basic to the ecumenical movement that dialogue and face-to-face contact, where misinterpretation is amenable to immediate correction, will highlight what Christians share in common and serve to minimize what keeps them apart. In these times when religion is struggling to make itself heard above the din of the secular city, it takes such dramatic events as Pope John's XXIII's *Pacem in terris* and Paul VI's appearance before the United Nations in New York to make us aware of the moral impact of one voice speaking for the entire Christian Church.

Andrew M. Greeley

Advantages and Drawbacks of a Centre of Communications in the Church

2. *Sociological Point of View*

THE social scientist is not equipped as a social scientist to discuss the theology of the papacy. But viewing the Church as a human organization from a sociological perspective, he is required to say that even if Christianity did not have a pope, it would have to invent one; that even if the papacy was not part of a divine institution of the Church, it still would have developed out of organizational necessity. It is built into the nature of any large human corporation that it have a symbolic leader, and when that organization is a sacred organization, it is practically inevitable that the symbolic leader will be a sacred symbol.[1] The papacy is not merely an essential sacred symbol for the Christian Church, it also is or at least can be an extraordinarily important institution for facilitating the proclamation of the Gospel and for speaking to the conscience of the world from the Christian perspective.

One must acknowledge that there have been times in the history of the Church, not excluding the present time, when there has been variation in the effectiveness of the leadership role of the papacy, though one hesitates to think of any period in the past when the papacy was more universally respected or when the pope had any greater moral influence in the world than did Pope John XXIII. The impact of the Johannine papacy in the world beyond the Church is ample evidence, if any were needed,

[1] As we shall point out later in this paper, to say that a leadership is symbolic is not to say that it has no power, but rather it is to assert that it has more power not less power than a leadership which is purely administrative.

of how important the papacy can be, even in a supposedly secularized modern world.

I. Types of Religious Leadership

We will speak first of the nature of religious leadership, and then of the nature of leadership in the modern world. There are many different forms of the religious charisma, but they all represent some sort of special contact with the sacred; some kind of extraordinary relationship with the transcendent that enables the possessor of the charisma to stand as a go-between, mediating between the sacred and the rest of the tribe. In addition to the shaman, Wach distinguishes nine other forms of religious leadership[2]:

(a) The Founder

This, of course, is the most important religious leader, the one who begins a religious tradition.

(b) The Reformer

While the reformer is not a man of the magnitude of the importance of the founder, and while he does not begin a new religious tradition, he does introduce tremendous new energies, and quite possibly a new direction, into old religious traditions.

(c) The Prophet

The prophetic charisma according to Wach implies "immediate communion with the deity, the intensity of which is more characteristic than its continuance". The prophet is pre-eminently a man who speaks, who interprets, though his interpretation, unlike that of the founder, does not introduce a new or vastly renovated tradition.

(d) The Seer

The principal difference between the prophet and the seer is that the seer's interpretation is likely to be delivered to a group of men who surround him as he sits under a tree, while the prophet's is likely to be delivered to a crowd which follows him down the road or which stands in awe as he storms into the

[2] Joachim Wach, *Sociology of Religion* (Chicago, 1944), pp. 343-69.

market-place. It is worth noting, however, that both the seer and the prophet *interpret* for their followers. The meaning of the ultimate interpretive schemes is not always clear in special sets of circumstances and, therefore, one must seek out someone who has "the words of life".

(e) *The Magician*

The magician is a man who can get things done for you. You approach him not so much when you are interested in finding interpretation or an explanation but when you want someone who understands how things go in the spirit world, to get results for you from the spirits. However, the magician's role is still an interpretative one. It is precisely his ability to interpret sacral, that is to say, ultimate reality that enables him to satisfy the requirements of his clients.

(f) *The Diviner*

The diviner is also a more practical man, but his concerns are more with what is going to happen than with producing results for clients. The diviner, then, is something of a "scientist" in that he has an elaborate methodology for developing his interpretive schemes.

(g) *The Saint*

The saint, on the other hand, interprets the ultimate for people not so much by what he knows but by who he is. The saint is the guru, the holy man.

(h) *The Priest*

The priest is, of course, pre-eminently the cultic man: the man who presides over worship. But the cultic function is merely the core of an extremely elaborate role much of which involves interpretation, and some of it extremely elaborate and abstract interpretation.

(i) *The "Religiosus"*

Finally, there is a man (or woman) who derives a kind of unofficial or quasi-official religious authority from his (or her) commitment to a special life of communion with God. It will be noted here, too, there is an interpretive role, though sometimes only an indirect one. For the *religiosus*, by the very example of his "good life", shows others how they ought to be living if they are to honour the ultimate interpretive scheme.

All nine of Wach's categories involve interpretive functions. The founder and the reformer explicate the ultimate nature of reality in terms of their own religious experience and collect followers around them precisely because to the followers that religious experience seems to be a normative interpretation of the ultimate. The seer, the prophet and the diviner are explicitly concerned with interpretation; and the priest must interpret the cultic lore, which is merely an elaboration of the ultimate meaning system of his people. The saint and the *religiosus* interpret reality for us by serving as exemplars of the "good life" which is the "ethos" side of one's ultimate "world view".

II. Religious Leadership in the Modern World

While it is possible for societies to dispense with interpreters of their world view, these societies have to be quite primitive. Once social reality becomes complex, interpretation is inevitably required. The religious leader is, in the final analysis, the man who understands the "meaning system" better than others. If the basic contention of this volume—that meaning systems are required today as much as they ever were—is valid, it would follow that sacred leadership is every bit as important as it ever was. The conventional wisdom, of course, is every bit as important as it ever was. The conventional wisdom, of course, denies such a conclusion and argues, rather, that the clergyman ought to find his validation in being "relevant"; engaging in political or social action or becoming a bargain basement psychoanalyst. Interpreting the ultimate, it is alleged, is no longer pertinent, because men no longer need the ultimate.

One can only respond that such an explanatory model has a very hard time coping with the emphasis of charisma in the new left and with the search for holy men among the mystics. May it also be noted in passing, it ignores the quasi-sacral role of some of the great charismatic leaders of the twentieth century for some of whom the modifier "quasi" could easily be eliminated: De

Gaulle, Churchill, Roosevelt, Hitler, Mao, Adenauer, Fidel, Ho, John Kennedy, Martin Luther King, John XXIII. These leaders were all men who spoke of "the nature of things" and who attracted vigorous, enthusiastic followers precisely because they were able to tap the deep roots of the ultimate convictions of their people.

I now wish to turn to a more detailed description of what I take to be the functions of leadership in the Church or, indeed, in any human organization.

(a) Symbolic Leadership

In a recent article in *Commentary*, Midge Dichter suggested that it was reactionary to wish to be governed by attractive people and deduced that the whole Kennedy cult of the 1960s was basically reactionary. This is the sort of superficial smartness that one has come to expect from intellectual journals. Reactionary or not, the human need for leaders who incarnate the goals, values and elan of an organization is powerful and probably permanent. An effective leader must be "transparent". That is to say, his commitment to the values and goals of the organization must be such that the members can see in him the personification of what the organization is striving for. What is required, one suspects, is not a special kind of personal attractiveness but rather a clear, enthusiastic and articulate commitment to goals. The great men of the sixties, such as John Kennedy and Martin Luther King, were not pied pipers; but they were men whose convictions and commitments were unmistakable. Man seems to need in his leaders evidence that they "really believe" the things they say and that they really have confidence that the goals they describe can be achieved. I do not believe that the mass media can "merchandise" this quality.

There is no room then in the symbolic leader for self-pity or hand-wringing, for indecisiveness or hedging of bets. He must have courage, wit, hope and the willingness to take risks. He must be able to channel energies and enthusiasms instead of trying to restrain them. He must, in John Kennedy's words, say, "Why not?" instead of "Why?" Midge Dichter, to the contrary notwithstanding, it seems most unlikely that either the need for or the availability of this sort of leader is going to be eliminated from modern society.

The symbolic leader plays both a prophetic and therapeutic role, which is to say he both challenges and comforts. He stirs his followers out of their lethargy, complacency and self-satisfaction. He is not satisfied with the way things are and he demands of those associated with him that they use the best of their talents. On the other hand, he is not a prophet in the sense of Amos denouncing or Jeremiah sitting on the edge of the city calling down imprecations. He is also able to comfort, to reassure, to strengthen, to support. If he says to his followers that certain things must be done, he also says they are capable of doing them. His prophecy is never such as to make his associates feel inadequate. Quite the contrary, his prophecy is designed to make them feel more adequate than they were before they heard the prophecy.

(b) *Ideological*

Precisely because he is in a leadership position, the leader is forced to see the "big picture", that is to say, he must be aware of both the overall needs of his organization and of the values and traditions which constitute the ideology of the organization. His associates are involved in their own specific tasks and needs and are not normally inclined to look beyond these immediate tasks and needs to the "big picture". It is a leader's role, then, precisely to prevent his associates turning in on themselves and their own immediate problems and preoccupations. He is *not* a man who provides answers—a relatively easy and quite futile task. He is rather a man whose assumption it is to ask the right questions, to point out the relationships between the group's values and the "big picture", which will force the other members of the group to think through their beliefs and their obligations. He poses problems, not solutions.

And he also rejects incomplete answers, that is to say, answers which do not take into account either the ideology of the organization or the reality of the problems it faces. Thus, the Kennedys rejected an answer to the Cuban missile crisis which would have involved a surprise attack on Cuba precisely because it was false to the American tradition. Similarly, one would suppose that a religious leader would reject any response to contemporary problems of sexuality which would ignore the need to respect human life. But, what I am suggesting is that the leader would ask the question: "What does our insight into the meaning of sexuality imply for our religious beliefs and behaviour?", and let his colleagues attempt to arrive at an answer instead of imposing one on his own initiative. It takes no great skill to provide answers, but to ask the right questions, to distinguish between answers that are adequate and answers that are inadequate, requires a great deal of skill. Unfortunately, we do not yet seem to have much of this skill in the Roman Church.

(c) *Interpersonal*

The leader realizes that in the complex world in which we live he can ill afford to lose any of the talents of the members of his group. He therefore must create an atmosphere in which there is the greatest possibility for his individual colleagues to develop their talents to the maximum. This means not only guaranteeing them the greatest degree of freedom possible within the group but also creating an atmosphere of harmony and social support among his colleagues. Basic to this, of course, is his obligation to protect the rights of members of the group but, also, he must do all that he can to see that the conflicts and the strains which exist among his various colleagues are honestly and openly worked out. Conflict and tension cannot be eliminated from the human condition but its negative effects can be minimized both by bringing conflicts into the open and by providing for everyone a sufficient amount of personal security so that every new conflict does not seem to be an attack on the core of one's personality.

The interpersonal skills that are required of the leader might be compared to the socio-emotional role traditionally attributed to the mother of the family for it has been assumed that the mother is the one who has been responsible for harmonizing difficulties, healing hurts, protecting rights and facilitating in development of talent. I would note, however, that in the best of modern families the father shares in the socio-emotional leadership just as a mother shares in the task-oriented leadership.

(d) *Organizational*

Despite the naïve romanticism of our young, and some of our not so young, no groups of human beings could function for very long unless there is organizational effort. The leader then either must be an administrator or see that administration gets done. Administration may be less important than symbolizing the goals and values in an organization or interpreting its ideology or creating an effective interpersonal environment. This does not mean that it is unimportant. Because some ecclesiastical leaders have, alas, equated administration with leadership does not mean that we can now have ecclesiastical groups in which administration is taboo.

The leader must, first of all, obtain the consent of his colleagues for the major decisions that the group makes. Effective authority is, in the final analysis, the ability to obtain consent. Just as it is easy to give answers, so it is easy to give orders. But orders and answers can be ignored particularly when one does not have a secular arm available to enforce them. However divine one may be persuaded one's power is, it still is a useless power unless it is accepted by those towards whom it is being directed. A leader who is not able to obtain the consent of a very large majority of his colleagues on a given policy matter has failed as a leader, no matter how noble the title he may claim. Not only, then, does the leader propose the right questions, but he also presides over the dialogue which will lead to a response to the questions. He realizes that everyone whose co-operation is necessary for the implementation of the decision ought to have some kind of participation in the making of the decision. If any substantial part of the membership is excluded from the decision-making then the chances of a successful implementation of the decision are minimal.

Secondly, the leader must preside over the implementation of the decision. He must direct and co-ordinate the activities of his colleagues in such a way that the maximum result is obtained in the minimum of effort. It is not, for example, necessary to convene a meeting of the whole group to determine whether stamps should be purchased (not, as happened in one convent I know, have a twenty-minute discussion each day before Mass as to what hymns were to be sung). The leader must see, in other words, to the "book-keeping" and "house-keeping" details. It is an onerous and perhaps thankless task, and his colleagues may grumble and complain about the need to be concerned over such details. Nevertheless, they would not grumble and complain much louder if the leader failed to arrange for the book-keeping and the house-keeping in such a way that the organizational climate of the group did not provide some stability and order.

Finally, the leader must see that the organization is arranged in such a way as to maximize pluriformity among the various subgroups within it. For just as the talents of the individuals are developed when they have the greatest possible amount of freedom, so the contribution of subgroups will be most effective when they, too, enjoy the greatest amount possible of initiative, responsibility and structural flexibility. Just as it would be disastrous for an organization if everybody behaved exactly the same, so it would be disastrous if each subgroup within the organization was under obligation to follow one, and only one model. Pluriformity is messy, inconvenient, and fits poorly on an organizational chart but, in its absence, vitality and variety and ingenuity and creativity vanish. Perhaps the worst thing about Max Weber's bureaucrats is that they are so uniform. Given the strain towards routinization and uniformity in the modern world, the leader preserves pluriformity only if he is willing to take positive action to promote, facilitate and guarantee variety and flexibility. He cannot assume, at least not in the present state in the evolution of the species, that pluriformity will take care of itself, but he can assume that the alternative to pluriformity is apathy.

III. The Functions of a Pope

If it is the role of religious leadership to give meaning, and if in the modern world leadership is to exercise the four functions that I have just described, and if the papacy is perceived as the supreme religious leadership position in the Christian Church, then it follows that the primary role of the papacy is to *interpret*, to speak to men, both Christian and non-Christian, of the meaning of reality and of events. The pope must, by his personal posture, by the sorts of questions he asks, by the atmosphere he creates in the Church and, last but not least, by the effectiveness of his administration, see that the Christian Church becomes more of the light on the mountain-top that it was destined to be—a light bearing witness to the Christian conviction that God is a God of Love and that his love is proclaimed by the quality of relationships that men have with one another.

As a symbol, the papacy must stand for conviction and confidence—conviction that the Suffering Servant had indeed become the Son of Man, and that through suffering and death man comes to resurrection. The pope must be the prime "celebrant" of Christianity, a man who presides over the joyous festivities that ought to mark the Christian conviction that life has triumphed over death. He ought to be the principal friend of that "band of brothers, that happy few" who constitute the community of Christ's followers. He should be the most open, the most loving, the most trusting of all Christians. His confidence in the Christian commitment, his openness to all men, his joy over the Good News, and his trust in the work of the Spirit must be *transparent*; they must shine forth in his words, in his actions, and in his whole style of leadership. The papacy which is occupied by a man of such transparent convictions will necessarily and inevitably be the most influential leadership position in the world without ever having to issue a single command or a single denunciation, a single warning or a single reproof. The papacy not occupied by such a man will, one very much fears, increasingly enjoy very little credibility. The days when a cult of personality could flourish in the Western world are long since past. The unsparing glare of the television camera and the unceasing, probing publicity of the world press make it impossible for the pope to hide behind the paraphernalia of his office. Who he is, what he stands for, what he believes in is unmercifully explored and unerringly recorded. In a world without television and instantaneous communication Pope John might not have lived long enough to have any impact at all; but in the world of TV and instant communication, the sort of man he was was known very quickly. He may have had his defects as an administrator, he may not have thought out too clearly the precise direction in which he wished the Church to go. The world recognized these facts and did not care, for it saw him as a man of faith and openness and trust; and also, perhaps necessarily, as a man of wit and laughter; the world asked for nothing more.

The papacy must ask the most probing and most challenging questions, questions which assume a perspective that must encompass the whole of the world. If all leaders must see the big picture, the pope must see the biggest picture of all, encompassing problems that run from New Zealand to Greenland; from Taos, New Mexico to Tanzania; from the Bering Straits to the Cape of Good Hope. He must see these problems against a cosmic background, the background of a vision concerned with the ultimate destiny of man and of the whole of the creation of which man is a part. To attempt merely to provide answers for specific problems against a background of such a gigantic world view seems hopelessly difficult. No man can be expected to have the knowledge or the insights of experience to provide such answers by himself. Even the special guidance of the Spirit could not be expected in the ordinary course of things to make up for the absolutely insurmountable problems of knowledge and information and insight such decisions would require.

But in another sense, providing answers is far too trivial a task for the pope; it is considerably less important than knowing what the right questions are and how to ask them. Groups and advisors can be assembled to bring to bear all the resources of scholarship and insight and information that are required for answers but these scholars lack direction and inspiration unless someone can address to them the proper questions. And, indeed, bishops, priests and Christian people of the world do not require detailed specific answers nearly as much as they require the challenge and the inspiration of the right question addressed in the right way to the right people at the right time. A papacy concerned with the art of asking questions rather than the service of providing answers is indeed a papacy heavily burdened with an extraordinarily difficult responsibility, but it is also a papacy with far more power than one which sees its responsibility to lie in answering questions. When one ponders the power and the influence the papacy could have if it saw its role as essentially one of asking the most challenging of questions, one is dazzled and overwhelmed. There is no office on earth that could be more important. If it does not at a given time in history enjoy the influence it ought to have, then the condition of the papacy must be accounted as a judgment on the condition of the whole Church.

The papacy must also play a "social-emotional" or a "comforting" role in the Church. The pope must be perceived as a man deeply concerned about the dignity, the integrity and the freedom of men everywhere in the world, and he must be particularly careful to see that the rights of no one in the Church are violated by other members of the Church. He must be something of a world-wide ombudsman or tribune of last recourse. He must see that rights are protected not only from abuse by official leaders, but also from violation by demagogues, manipulators and charlatans (breeds of men which in our day of increased religious enthusiasm are once more flourishing). The pope must see it as his task to call forth the best in the talents, energies and the enthusiasms of the members of the Church and of all Christians. He must stand for harmony in a world of polarization, for dialogue in a world of demagogic rhetoric, for negotiation and consensus in a world of confrontation, for peaceful and persistent change in a world where empty nonsense about revolution is spoken even by theologians who ought to know better. The pope, in other words, must stress those things that bind men together, not only among members of the Church, but also among the whole human race. He must be particularly careful to see that the papacy is not a device of institution. If it should be true, as has recently been said, that the papacy is the biggest obstacle to unity among Christians, then one suspects that it is because of a profound misunderstanding of the role of the papacy, for leadership ought to be unifying and not divisive.

Finally, the pope ought to be an administrator. While administration is less important than the other three roles, it is none the less essential. Unless the technical aspects of administration are provided for, an atmosphere of order and system that will make it possible for the other three roles to be exercised will not survive. The pope as administrator could be seen as the co-ordinator in the centre of communication among the national and local churches. He must preside over an extensive "research and development" staff which is available both to challenge and facilitate the work of the local and national churches. He must see that resources of personnel and finances are available where they are most needed. It is frequently said that one of the major advantages of the Vatican Council was that bishops from one part of the world came to understand the problems and perspectives of other parts of the world. The papacy should be concerned at all times with making as much of this experience available to as many Christians as possible.

If the pope is to be an effective administrator, he probably will need a larger staff than he has at the present time rather than a smaller one. It is not, therefore, a question of abolishing the Roman Curia or even modernizing it, but rather of making available to the pope through the Curia the best possible resources of research and planning and of keeping the pope informed of the problems and possibilities of the whole world. A Curia which coordinates and facilitates communication, makes available the resources of research and development, and keeps the pope informed about the "big picture" is not a Curia with less power than the present one, but, I would submit, a Curia with more power.

It is, I think, necessary for the papacy to be sacred. As I have pointed out elsewhere, it is simply false to think that man has evolved to a new state where he no longer needs the sacred. The sacred and the secular are correlates and not opposites. A leadership position is effective in the modern world to the extent that it appeals not merely to man's reason, not merely to his respect for expertise, but also to his primordial passions, to his emotions, and to the affective dimension of his personality. It is not a question of whether the papacy is a sacred role or not, but of what the most effective methods are for assuring that the papacy's sacral nature be pertinent to the religious needs of man. Pope John was an extraordinarily informal and unceremonious man and, yet, few men have brought to the papacy a more meaningful sacred. There are those who would abolish all the ceremony and the ritual of the papacy and would argue that the pope should go about dressed in a business suit like any other citizen of the modern world. In my judgment it does not matter much what kind of clothes the pope wears but it does very much matter, I think, that there be ceremony in the papacy to stress both the continuity of the office with the past and also its unique position in the contemporary

8—c.

world. The American presidency, the chief executive position of a nation with a heavy ideological commitment to equalitarianism, is none the less surrounded by an impressive and, on the whole, effective ceremonial ritual. Similarly, if one compares the position of the general secretary of the World Council of Churches with the position of the Archbishop of Canterbury, one is forced to conclude that Canterbury, precisely because there is ceremony and tradition attached to his office, does appeal, all other things being equal, far more effectively to the total personality of his followers than does the very bureaucratic role of the general secretary of the WCC. One could say that of course the general secretary was not intended to be a charismatic role, to which the only appropriate reply would be, so much the worse for the World Council of Churches.

I would emphasize in conclusion that I am not suggesting a watering down of the powers of the papacy. On the contrary, I would insist most strongly that the sociological view of the papacy expressed in this article is a view that sees the papacy as the most powerful leadership position in the entire world, powerful precisely because it is a religious and spiritual leadership more than it is a political one. The pertinent question to be asked about the papacy is how its power and influence might be most effectively exercised. One would be less than honest if one said that one thought the credibility and influence of the papacy was at the present time extraordinarily high. One would also be far too pessimistic if one concluded that it would be practically impossible for the papacy to become in fact as well as in theory the most important leadership position in the world once again. Quite the contrary, I should think that it ought to be relatively easy.

Stylianos Harkianakis

Can a Petrine Office be Meaningful in the Church?
1. *A Greek Orthodox Reply*

FOR the Orthodox theologian, there are two aspects to the question concerning the Petrine office in the Church. On the one hand, there is the problem of assessing theologically the idea of primacy as such and, on the other, the theological problem of the primacy of Rome. The idea of a primacy as such has never been alien to Orthodox thought and is still acceptable today, whereas the primacy of Rome is still, for the Orthodox theologian, a real obstacle on the way to Christian unity. In the language of inter-confessional theology, the term "primacy of Rome" does not imply a priority or precedence, which is open to a more precise definition, of the Church of Rome within the Church as a whole. On the contrary, it has the unequivocal meaning of the primacy of the bishop of Rome as it exists today in its fully developed state and as precisely defined by the First Vatican Council as an infallible teaching and jurisdictional authority.

As the historical circumstances which conditioned and led up to this development in the Roman Church are very well known today and have even been openly admitted by Roman Catholic theologians and historians themselves,[1] it should be possible for me to dispense with the usual historical survey in this short article, which is written from the point of view of systematic theology.[2] This does not, however, mean that I regard the

---

[1] In this context, one has only to think of the variety of books and articles written about this subject by, for example, Y. Congar, H. Jedin, H. Küng, W. Kasper and others.

[2] A comprehensive survey of the principal stages in the development of

historical development of the idea of the primacy of Rome and
the historical argument in theology generally as irrelevant or questionable. It is all the more important to stress this because it is so
necessary to assess the historical aspect as distinct from the systematic aspect in theology.[3] The systematic theologian at least has
to try to distinguish clearly between these two aspects, because
a failure to make this distinction and an uncritical confusion of
the *status viatoris* with the *status gloriae* is bound to lead, with
an almost mathematical certainty, to rigidity and triumphalism
in the life of the Church.

Orthodox theologians have never really disputed the existence
of a primacy of the Church of Rome within the Church as a
whole. What they have not failed to notice, however, is that the
Roman Catholic view of the essential nature of this primacy and
the attempts made by Catholic theologians to justify it have
always given rise to violent controversy, not only between East
and West, but also in the West itself. What this conflict expresses
above all for the Orthodox theologian is a fundamental ecclesiological misunderstanding, the full extent and significance of
which has only become apparent since the First Vatican Council.

I. A Monarchical Church?

The questions which are usually asked in this context are, for
example, whether Peter was really the first among the apostles or
not and whether the bishop of Rome is really the only successor
of this first among the apostles or not. These questions, however,
have to be answered, from the point of view of systematic theology at least, by placing them within a much more radical framework, namely that of the fundamental question: *Is the structure
of the Christian Church in the light of the gospel, monarchical*

---

the doctrine of primacy in the history of the Church will be found in
J. Meyendorf, *Ithiki kai Thriskeutiki Engyklopaideia* (Athens, 1966),
Vol. X, 702–14; see also S. Harkianakis, *The Infallibility of the Church
in Orthodox Theology* (Athens, 1965), pp. 92–128. Another important contribution is *Der Primat des Petrus in der orthodoxen Theologie* (Zürich,
1961), edited by N. Affanassieff and others.

[3] For the validity of this theological argument, see J. Ratzinger's article
on primacy ("Primat") in *Lexikon für Theologie und Kirche*, Vol. VIII,
2nd edn., 761.

or collegial? This question is undoubtedly radical because it is asked, on the one hand, with the whole Christian people in mind and, on the other, from the point of view of what the Lord himself taught, that is, in the light of the gospel of Christ as a whole.[4]

We may go further and say that, if the structure of the Church is conditioned by and subject to the norm of the gospel of Christ, we must base our argument less on the isolated descriptions or ideas of the Church which occur almost accidentally in the New Testament and which do not in any case always agree exactly with each other and more on the general spirit of the words of the Lord as the origin of those images of the Church. That essentially new element in the teaching of the Lord which distinguishes it from the teaching contained in all the religions and ideologies that have so far arisen in the history of man is the doctrine of the Trinity. This is the *differentia specifica* of Christianity.[5]

In the light of this faith in the Trinity, the Christian teaching about God's being, the creation of the world and the cosmic and metaphysical order of the universe has always been different from that of other religions and ideologies. It has, in a word, been trinitarian. The idea of the Trinity is central, not only in the doctrine of the Christian Church, but also—and in the first place—in the teaching of the Lord himself. If this is so, then surely it is bound to inspire the whole task of the Christian Church to give a new structure to the created world. This brings us to the question of the relationship between the doctrine of the Trinity and Christology.

II. The Fundamental Question of the Relationship between Unity and Multiplicity

At the most holy moment of his life on earth and just before he left this world, Christ prayed to his Father and at the same time expressed his most fervent desire: "I do not pray for these

---

[4] This should certainly not be thought of in the Protestant sense of *sola Scriptura*. In using the expression "gospel of the Lord" here, I mean the whole teaching of the gospel living in the Church and not simply the pure "letter" of Scripture.

[5] See S. Harkianakis, "Die Trinitätslehre Gregors von Nazianz", in *Kleronomia*, Vol. I, Part I, pp. 83–102.

only, but also for those who believe in me through their word, that they may be one; even as thou, Father, art in me, and I in thee" (John 17. 20 f.).

It is perhaps symptomatic that, in an attempt to stress the holiness of the ecumenical intention, these words are quoted nowadays at almost every meeting between Christians of different denominations. Yet we usually think very little about these important words afterwards. The phrase "that they may be one" expresses the practical and immediate aims of ecumenism better than the idea which follows, namely "as thou, Father, art in me. . . .". But these words become even more meaningful perhaps if we remember that this exemplary mode of unity within the Trinity is the basic presupposition for the unity of the Church which we hope will be achieved. The importance of the whole passage is even further emphasized by the fact that Christ did not have a definite group of people, such as the apostles, in mind when he spoke these words, but rather all those who believed in him and would believe in him throughout history. It is this universal validity of the moral principle that is expressed here which gives it its distinctive and normative character. This is why it must constitute the basic and first ecclesiological premiss for all theological thinking at all times.

It is clear therefore that there must be a direct relationship between the doctrine of the Trinity and ecclesiology, a relationship expressed in fact in the striking parallel that exists between the fundamental theological questions of the Church's trinitarian and ecclesiological teaching. If the inner interrelationships that exist in the historical development of dogma in the Church and have existed since the earliest times are borne in mind, it is not difficult to recognize that the main problem confronting all theological thinking throughout the history of the Church has always been the same—the fundamental question of the relationship between unity and multiplicity.

In the first centuries of Christianity, this fundamental question arose in connection with God's being. Later, it arose in connection with the essence of the Church. The question as to how God could be thought of as three persons while at the same time still remaining one God was superseded by the question as to how the Church, which was founded by Christ as one Church, could at the same time exist as many different individual churches or, alternatively, how the many different individual members of the Church could at the same time constitute only one body, the body of the Lord.

If the parallel between the two doctrines that I have mentioned does in fact hold good, we can now draw the obvious conclusion. Before stating this in concrete form, however, we must anticipate a misgiving which does, at first sight, seem to be justified. It is this. Is it legitimate or, even worse, is it not positively blasphemous to compare the life of the Church with God's intertrinitarian life? I would give the following answer to this question. It is true that this is only an analogy. It is, however, a very profound analogy and it is all the more important and indeed legitimate to make it because it is required by the Lord himself. What should above all not be forgotten in this context, however, is the authentic Christian teaching that man's ultimate goal is nothing less than the well-known *theosis* of the Greek Fathers of the Church.

The main conclusion which we may draw from this analogy is that we may legitimately apply the doctrine of the Trinity as it was developed in the first ecumenical councils of the still undivided Church to ecclesiology. To express this in a more concrete form, we may say this. Just as the idea of *homoousia* in the trinitarian dilemma does not violate the independence of the individual persons of the Trinity, so too does the idea of the unity of the Church in the ecclesiological problem not violate the independence of the individual churches or of the individual persons belonging to those churches. What is more, just as the idea of a *subordinatio* was not accepted in the life of the Trinity, so too has this idea to be excluded from the life of the Church.

These, then, are, very briefly, the fundamental principles which can be derived from the Church's teaching about the Trinity as applied as norms to the ecclesiological problem.

III. THE FIRST BISHOP

The question as to whether the primacy of Rome, as defined by the First and unfortunately also by the Second Vatican Council, really has any place at all in this idea of the Church has therefore to be answered with an emphatic "no". This does not, however, imply a complete denial of any primacy within the Orthodox Church. By this, I mean that acceptance of the principle of synodal collegiality leads to acknowledgment of one bishop as the first among the bishops, in other words, it leads to according primacy to him, not, it has to be admitted, in the sense of a *pontifex maximus*, but rather in the sense of *primus inter pares*.

This idea of a primacy has been formulated in a very remarkable way in the 34th of the so-called Apostolic Canons,[6] which takes the whole context of "power structures" in the Church into consideration: "The bishops of every people are to acknowledge the first among them and regard him as the head".

This canon goes on to say that the first among the bishops cannot do anything without the opinion of all the others, and the others cannot do anything without the opinion of the first. The theological justification for this is that "it is only in this way that harmony can be achieved, so that God is glorified through the Lord in the Holy Spirit, God the Father, the Son and the Holy Spirit".

Two fundamental ecclesiological principles, then, are stressed in this canon, the first being *autocephaly* and the second *collegiality*. Each is correlative with the other.[7] This therefore is the situation in the local church, which has recently come to be interpreted by several Orthodox theologians as a *eucharistic ecclesiology*.[8] Even the simple idea that the ecumenical Church on earth began as a local church and did not develop into a group of several local churches until a later stage in history leads us to the same conclusion, namely that there must be one bishop among all the bishops of the whole Church who is *primus inter pares* in the sense outlined above.[9]

The bishop of Rome was, of course, acknowledged to be the "first among equals" while the Church was still undivided, although it is not necessary or possible to go into the reasons for

---

[6] See H. Alivizatos, *Hoi Hieroi Kanones* (Athens, 1949), pp. 143-4.

[7] See S. Harkianakis, "Über die geganwärtige Situation der orthodoxen Kirche", *Kyrios* 6 (1966), p. 229.

[8] For the possibilities and the limitations of this eucharistic ecclesiology, see S. Harkianakis, *Über die Unfehlbarkeit der Kirche in der orthodoxen Theologie* (Athens, 1965), p. 97 ff.

[9] See O. Cullmann, *Petrus-Jünger-Apostel-Märtyrer* (Zürich, 1952), p. 255.

this here.[10] So long as he regarded his primacy as the primacy of a "first among equals", it was possible for him to express an opinion of decisive importance in matters of concern to the whole Church and to be respected by everyone. In this way, he was really able to perform an essential service in the Church as a whole. As soon as he began, however, to regard his episcopal power as basically different from the power of all the other bishops, it was no longer possible for him to remain in communion with the Orthodox Church.

All the bishops participate in the *apostolic succession* and all the local churches are for this reason in communion with each other. By regarding the *Petrine succession* and not the apostolic succession of all the bishops as the origin and basis of this power, the pope isolated himself not only from the community of the bishops, but also from the whole Church. Seen in this light, it was quite logically consistent for the First Vatican Council to define the decisions made by the pope *ex cathedra* as irreversible *ex sese, non autem ex consensu Ecclesiae*. It was also only to be expected that the Second Vatican Council was unable to change this situation in any way.[11]

The Church is, however, a community and if any person, no matter who he is, isolates himself from the other members of that community if only for a moment, then he is automatically placed in the situation of original sin and can only be compared with a "monad without windows".

It is therefore not primarily for canonical reasons, but rather for deeply soteriological reasons that the synodal structure of the Church is so highly valued in Orthodox circles.[12] None the less, both reasons are inwardly very closely connected in Orthodox thought and both lead to a radical rejection of the primacy of Rome in matters of jurisdiction and in the question of infallibility.

[10] See G. Konidaris, *General Church History* (Athens, 1957), pp. 239–40.
[11] See S. Harkianakis, *The Constitution on the Church of the Second Vatican* (Thessalonica, 1969), pp. 171–86.
[12] See P. Duprey's well-informed article, "La structure synodale de l'Eglise dans la théologie orientale", in *Proche-Orient-Chrétien* (1970), pp. 123–45.

Translated by David Smith

Paul Evdokimov

Can a Petrine Office be Meaningful in the Church?
2. *A Russian Orthodox Reply*

I. THE THREE MINISTRIES

FOR a valid reply to the question, one only has to go back to St Paul: "Let everything be done fittingly and *in order* in all the churches of the saints". In the visible Church, it is precisely the "Petrine ministry" that safeguards the institutional order, but, having said this, we must be clear what we mean by "Petrine ministry".

From among the Twelve, St Peter is the *protos*. His primacy, clearly, is not a primacy of power, but one of authority. The Eastern Fathers commenting on Matthew 16. 18 stress the fact that Peter is the "rock" of the Church *to the extent that* he confesses his faith in Jesus Christ the Son of God. And all those who imitate Peter and his confession inherit the same promise. More particularly, the bishops are invested with a special charism of proclamation of the true faith, and this is why they are *ex officio* representatives of the Petrine ministry.

The Church came into being on the day of Pentecost and in the first eucharist celebrated by the apostles. It was certainly Peter who presided over this first meal, and this is another sense in which he is the "rock", the eucharistic foundation-stone of the Church. Without this "perpetuated rock", the rock of the power of bishops to celebrate the eucharist, the Church has no existence.

But the Petrine ministry has to achieve a balance with the other ministries. Liturgically, the Church celebrates three apostolic leaders: John, Peter and Paul. Paul, who "stole" into the number of the apostles, represents the ministry of events, the prophetic

ministry of the people of God, of "apostolic men". John's confession in the Prologue of his gospel parallels that of Peter; he is
the one "whom Jesus loved" and who predicts his mysterious
destiny. The horizontal Petrine ministry is rooted in the vertical
Johannine ministry, the Church John perpetuated. It is this ministry that Orthodoxy gives pride of place in its spirituality, expressed in the eschatological maximalism of monasticism (consider the role of Mount Athos and the *startzi*), in the doxology
of the liturgy, and in the anthropology of deification and contem-
plation of the mysteries.

The Church, the Body of Christ, is not a juridical notion, but
a living organism of a *theandric* character. Its visible structure
may be controlled by canon law, but this is never autonomous,
being subordinate to the mystery of grace and life. Any definition of the Petrine ministry must take account of its context in
the other ministries. We must not fall into the clericalism of
hypostasizing the Petrine ministry on its own, nor the prophetic
anti-clericalism of taking the Pauline ministry alone, but aim for
an equilibrium of the three—Petrine, Pauline and Johannine—in
the image of the Trinity.

II. The Petrine Ministry of Bishops

The consensus of tradition agrees on the power of the keys
being given to all the apostles. St Irenaeus speaks of the apostolic
succession seating every bishop on the one and only throne of
Christ, since every local Church possesses the same fullness of
grace. The same ecclesiology is visible in St Cyprian, writing of
the *Cathedra Petri*: all the bishops, each in his own Church, sit
on the same throne. Even in Byzantium, nevertheless, Rome enjoyed particular prestige in memory of the leaders Peter and Paul,
and by virtue of its position as capital of the Empire. Nil Cabasilas
writes: "The Pope is bishop of Rome and the first among the
bishops" (P.G. 49, 701 CD). This does not imply a juridical
power of domination over the others, but a *care* exercised for the
common good is a very precise canonical setting. As the Catholic
historian Mgr Batiffol remarks with perfect objectivity: "The
authority of Rome is an authority of first rank, but there is nothing to suggest that the East has ever regarded it as being of divine

right" (*Cathedra Petri*, p. 75). During the Council of 869–70, Zachary of Chalcedon gave accurate expression to the Eastern view: "The canons command the patriarchs. So if they fail to regulate their conduct according to the canons, we refuse to follow them."

The Church only recognizes three ranks of hierarchy. There is no power above that of the bishop, no charism of super-episcopal, supreme primacy. There may be purely administrative differences between them, but from the charismatic point of view, all bishops are perfectly equal; there is no super-bishop, no *episcopus episcoporum*. That there is no power higher than that of the bishop in his diocese is a basic principle in the East.

III. Eucharistic Ecclesiology

The most ancient ecclesiology, which we call "eucharistic", talks of "the Church of God which is in Corinth", or "in Rome": that is, it sees the whole Church in every local Church. This is because the eucharist is not a part of Christ, but Christ whole and entire. In the same way, the local Church is not part of the *Una Sancta*, but its full manifestation in that place, the people of God reunited in their bishop. This conception necessarily excludes the idea of a power over the Church and its bishop, since such a power would be a power over Christ himself, each Church being the *totus Christus*, and such a thing is impossible.

All the same, fullness does not close in on itself, but opens out, and it is only in agreement and communion with all the others that a local Church can be identified as the Church of God, because unity belongs to the Church and not the Churches: each and all together form the One, Holy, Catholic and Apostolic Church. The rule laid down in the first Council, that a bishop must be ordained by two or three other bishops, expresses this communion, catholicity, *sobornost*, clearly: there is no subordination to any power above that of the new bishop. Once he has been ordained, it is he who immediately presides at the eucharist, as local "primate".

IV. Episcopal Collegiality and the Councils

The fact of the local Church presupposes the collegiality of all bishops. Bishops come together on a regional basis above all, to elect a new bishop, or to attend a provincial synod. Certain sees came to possess a more marked authority—vested in the Church, never in the person of its bishop, and strictly limited still by canonical boundaries. So the Fathers established an absolute rule that there could only be one bishop in each local community, and only one synod or council in each province. On principle, patriarchs and metropolitans never intervened in the internal affairs of the Churches dependent on them, except in cases where the canons had been transgressed or their advice had been sought. In disputes, recourse was had to collegiality in the shape of synods, and in cases of doctrinal debate, to collegiality in the shape of Ecumenical Councils. Yet the Council never became a power *over* the Churches, but a witness to their identity; its voice was the voice of each and every one of them, speaking not above the Church, but *in* it, and expressing its identity, agreement and communion.

V. "Primus inter Pares"

The analogy between apostolic collegiality and episcopal collegiality conditions the relationship between each ecclesial province and a "first" among the bishops, their "primate". The thirty-fourth Apostolic Canon states: "It behoves the bishops of each people to know who is the first among them and to do nothing outside their own Church without first having discussed it with him. . . . But neither should the first do anything without having discussed it with all the others." The ninth canon of the Council of Antioch distinguishes between the jurisdictional power of the local bishop and the function of the primate, which it calls "solicitude". The primate presides at the provincial synod and watches over ecclesiastical order, but without exercising any power as such over the bishops of his province. He is a bond of the communion in which every bishop participates. So he has no power to dominate, but a privilege of co-ordinating, advising and witnessing, and this combined with a reciprocal interdependence of all the bishops. He is in no way "supreme pontiff" but, as the Council of Carthage puts it, *episcopus primae sedis*.

Besides the regional primates, there is a universal primacy, the centre of unanimity of all the Churches, exercising a "solicitude", a care for the unity of faith, mission and life; the deep conscious-ness of the Church "spread throughout the earth, but living as if in one house", as St Irenaeus puts it.

VI. The Image-bearer of the Dogma of the Trinity

Orthodox ecclesiology is built on the dogma of the Trinity. The third Apostolic Canon defines the structure of the Church as the image of the Trinity. It is on this level that the Petrine ministry takes on its full meaning, in harmony with the Pauline and Johannine ministries. The 1848 encyclical of the Oriental Patriarchs declares that "the guardian of faith is the whole people of the Church", including the episcopate.

In the divine life, the Father assures unity without breaking the perfect equality of the Three, which excludes any form of submission, and is a magnificent demonstration of the Father as *He who presides in the love of the Trinity*. So in this image, there is within the communion of Churches, in which each is "the Church of God" by virtue of the fullness of its episcopal eucharist, one who presides in love. This is the particular charism attaching to the authority of honour whose aim is to *care for* the unity of all: a charism of love in the image of the heavenly Father, and for this very reason devoid of all jurisdictional power over the others. The "primate", as bishop of his diocese, exercises the Petrine ministry, but as *primus inter pares* the Petrine min-istry clearly gives place to the *Johannine ministry*.

Translated by Paul Burns

Arthur M. Allchin

Can a Petrine Office be Meaningful in the Church?

3. *An Anglican Reply*

I. The Office of the Bishop as Petrine Ministry

IT would be tempting for an Anglican to answer this question quite simply with the word, "Yes, a Petrine ministry can and does have significance in the Church; we see this ministry in the office of the bishop." Such an answer, over-simplified though it would be, would at least start from what Anglicans would regard as the right place. "Under the Spirit's guiding . . . the chief source of authority and leadership in the Church came to be vested in one who is himself a representative person—not in a committee, nor in a written constitution, but in a representative person. The bishop is one who expresses in his office both the representative and personal character of the Church's ministry, which in its turn continues the ministry of *the* Representative Person, Christ, the Proper Man." In such an office, "which is representative in that it addresses itself to all human concerns and activities, personal in that it is carried on by personal dealing as between man and man . . . the meaning of the gospel, and the structure of the Church are embodied".[1]

During the ten or more years since these words were spoken at an episcopal consecration, Anglicans have been attempting to rethink this question, in the light of the events of the present time. They are increasingly unwilling to deny the genuine oversight exercised by ministries called "non-episcopal". They are

[1] T. G. A. Baker, "The Office of a Bishop", in *Theology*, LXII, 466 (1959), pp. 147–8.

beginning, as we shall see, to consider more seriously, the genuine oversight exercised by the ministry called papal. But they continue firmly attached to their belief in the significance of the episcopal office. It stands, they believe, for the essential personal and sacramental nature of the Church as a communion of faith, service and worship. The Lambeth Conference of 1968 declared "the service of the bishop has its centre in the liturgical and sacramental life of the Church.... It is developed in his work of teaching and safeguarding the faith. . . . It reaches out in service and witness and prophetic word to the life of the human community as a whole."[2] Systematic theological reflection, good canon law, efficient administrative machinery are all highly desirable for the Church. But in times of need or persecution they may fall away, revealing the essential structure of a community united around the person of one who represents the Lord who took the form of a servant, of one who stands firm in the succession of Peter's confession of faith and repentance. "The bishop is called to exercise an authority which is rooted in the authority of the risen Christ."[3]

So in the words of William Temple, the greatest Archbishop of Canterbury of this century, and amongst the greatest pioneers of the movement towards unity, "When I consecrate a godly and well-learned man to the office and work of a bishop in the Church of God, I do not act as a representative of the Church if by that is meant the whole number of contemporary Christians; but I do act as the ministerial instrument of Christ in his body the Church. The authority by which I act is his, transmitted through his apostles and those to whom they committed it; I hold it neither from the Church, nor apart from the Church, but from Christ in the Church."[4]

An apostolic and Petrine ministry exists in the Church. It is shared by the whole college of bishops. It is not the exclusive prerogative of any one See. To say anything else seems, from the Anglican point of view, to limit the universality of God's grace, and the freedom of the action of the Spirit. The writings of

[2] *The Lambeth Conference 1968: Resolutions and Reports* (London, 1968), p. 108.   [3] *Ibid.*
[4] See A. M. Ramsey, *The Gospel and the Catholic Church* (London, 1964), pp. 229–30.

Anglican theologians from the seventeenth century onwards show a striking similarity at this point to those of the spokesmen of Eastern Orthodoxy since the later Middle Ages.[5] "Christ is his Church's monarch, and the Holy Ghost his deputy", wrote King James I in 1606, doubtless advised by his most competent theologians. There is a necessity to make the clearest possible distinction between the headship of Christ over the Church, and the position both of the bishop within his diocese, and of the first bishops within the college of bishops.[6]

II. THE FIRST IN THE COLLEGE

Having said this however we may well recognize the possibility that there should be a first among the bishops, and that in fact the Bishop of Rome alone has claim to this position. To quote James I again, "Let him, in God's Name, be Primus Episcopus *inter omnes episcopos*, and *Princeps Episcoporum*, so it be not otherwise than Peter was *Princeps Apostolorum*."[7] The Anglican participants in the Malines Conversations declared, "From the beginnings of Church history a primacy and leadership among all the bishops has been recognized as belonging to the Bishop of Rome". One of the consequences of this recognition is that "the Pope can claim to occupy a position in regard to all other bishops which no other bishop claims to occupy in regard to him".[8] At the same time a study of history shows that "the exercise of that primacy has in time past varied . . . ; and it may do so again". This possibility of variation, which has become a practical rather than a theoretical possibility in the last decade was welcomed by the Lambeth Conference of 1968, which recognized the papacy as an historic reality, whose role was still in

[5] Cf. J. Meyendorff, *The Primacy of Peter in the Orthodox Church* (London, 1963), pp. 19–29.

[6] This was done with admirable clarity by Patriarch Maximos IV in an intervention in the second session of Vatican II. See Y. Congar, H. Küng and D. O'Hanlon (eds.), *Council Speeches of Vatican II* (London, 1964), pp. 47–9.

[7] See D. W. Allen and A. M. Allchin, "Primacy and Collegiality: an Anglican View", in A. M. Ramsey (ed.), *Lambeth Essays on Unity* (London, 1969), pp. 6–23.

[8] G. K. A. Bell (ed.), *Documents on Christian Unity, Second Series* (London, 1930).

9—C.

process of development, and saw this subject as one calling for urgent joint study by all involved with the question of Christian unity.[9]

So far we have looked at this question in the light of Anglican tradition. We have seen, on the one hand, the conviction that Christ is Lord, and the Holy Spirit is active in Churches at present separated from one another, and not in communion with Rome. We have also seen the conviction that the one college of bishops, which inherits "the apostolic calling, responsibility and authority" (Lambeth, 1968) still exists, despite the fact that its members are not in communion with one another. All this necessarily implies serious differences with the definitions of papal primacy made at Vatican I and reaffirmed at Vatican II. On the other hand we have seen a willingness to recognize a form of papal primacy which would allow the Pope to be first among the bishops, in a way analogous to that in which Peter was first among the apostles.

III. A Centre of Unity

Have such considerations from the past any relevance for the present and the future? Yes, both ways. On the one side, in a world which is rapidly becoming one, it is vitally necessary for the Christian communities throughout the world to have a centre of unity to which all may gather. The constant inner pressure towards unity, inherent in the very nature of the Gospel, is reinforced by most evident external pressures, social, economic and political. An effective Petrine office, to sustain, encourage, coordinate and unify is vitally needed. Each bishop is himself a representative person, dealing personally, as man to man, with his fellow Christians in the Church in which he presides. Each bishop is also a member of a universal communion or college of bishops, which has need of an apostolic president, so that it may be a true communion of persons, and not merely a piece of administrative machinery.

But on the other side, it is also evident that the Church which is now freed from the geographical and cultural bounds of the old Christendom, and living everywhere in a world of rapid

[9] *Op. cit.*, pp. 137-8.

social and technological change, a world which if it is becoming unified is also ineradicably pluralist, will need to be open, flexible, diversified and free in ways hitherto scarcely dreamed of. The new and creative energies necessary for the restatement and re-presentation of the mystery of Christ in so many unprecedented human, social and intellectual situations will need to find in the Petrine ministry, not a repressive or anxious authoritarianism, but the genuine authority of a father who causes and enables things to grow. The sudden glimpse of such a true paternity in John XXIII fired the Christian world, far beyond the obedience of Rome, with a new vision of what the Petrine office of Rome was meant to be. Despite the hesitations which have followed since 1963, that vision has not wholly faded. As throughout the whole Church there is a recovery of the New Testament meaning of office as service, and of the New Testament understanding of communion as involving mutual confidence and shared responsi-bility, so it will become clearer to us how, in the growing unity of the body, the specific calling of the first among the bishops is to be lived and understood.

Heinrich Ott

Can a Petrine Office be Meaningful in the Church?

4. *A Protestant Reply*

THE idea of a "Petrine office", in other words, of a universal episcopate of Christianity, makes a strange, unaccustomed impression on the Protestant theologian. It is, moreover, from the historical point of view, a highly charged question, because of the polemics directed by the first Protestant reformers against the pope as the one claiming to carry out the function of Peter in the Church. Even though it has not been entirely neutralized, however, the question has undoubtedly become much less highly charged because of the new attitude brought about by the Second Vatican Council and the pope who opened that Council.

If the question is asked in such cautious theological language as it is here—Can a Petrine office be meaningful in the Church? —the Protestant theologian can certainly feel encouraged to think seriously about it without any desire to engage in polemics and, in order to forestall any possible polemics, to give a very positive answer.

Expressed in this way, the question is general enough to give the theologian attempting to answer it a great deal of latitude. The question is not, for example: "Does 'the Church' (in other words, the 'true Church') imply a Petrine office?" Nor is it: "Is a Petrine office necessary in the Church, so that the Church may be the 'true Church'?" What is more, the question refers to "*a* Petrine office", in other words, it does not refer necessarily to that Petrine office which the pope claims to carry out. Nor does it necessarily mean the office or service carried out by an individual person—according to the wording of the question, it might quite well mean a body or group of people such as a synod.

I. "PLACET IUXTA MODUM"

In the light of all these suppositions, the Protestant theologian can respond to the question and indeed provide an answer to it with a *placet iuxta modum*. This *iuxta modum* relates to the traditional presuppositions on the part of the one who asks the question and is conditioned by the original situation in which Protestantism first arose. This was, of course, a fundamental protest against all forms of mediation which kept men in a state of dependence and immaturity and this protest was made in the name of the believer's freedom of conscience which, the reformers insisted, could only be bound to God. If a Petrine office is to be at all meaningful in the Church, then the whole question of the believer's freedom of conscience, which is original and based on the reality of God, is intimately involved.

We must, however, first of all define exactly what is meant by Petrine office here. In order to do this, we have to go back to the basic structures of this concept in Roman Catholic theology. Simply to define this concept independently and without reference to its traditional definition in Roman Catholic theology would be to miss the whole point of this attempt to answer the question from the Protestant point of view, in other words, to engage in dialogue with the papal Church.

The basic structures of the Roman Catholic concept of the Petrine office can be found without difficulty in the Constitution *Pastor aeternus* of the First Vatican Council. Several of the scriptural passages quoted here give a clear indication of the direction in which the Constitution points. Jesus' commandment that Peter should feed his lambs and look after his sheep (John 12. 15) shows that the First Vatican Council thought of the office of Peter as a pastoral service. The quotation from Luke's gospel, "I have prayed for you that your faith may not fail; and when you have turned again, strengthen your brethren" (Luke 22. 32), indicates that the Petrine office was, in the opinion of the Fathers of the Council, to be at the service of the continuity of faith in the Church.

Finally, there is the Matthaean passage referring to the rock on which the Church is founded (Matt. 16. 18 ff.). This is a clear sign that the Petrine office was regarded as a guarantee of the lasting character and of the unity of the Church. These three basic structures—the pastoral service of Peter, the service to provide continuity of faith and the service to guarantee the perpetuity and unity of the Church—can be thought of together as forming the theological foundation of the Vatican doctrine of "infallibility". The pastoral office, in order to guarantee the effective continuity and unity of the Church, has to be able to be expressed in directives that are specifically binding *sui generis*.

If its basic structures are in fact as I have outlined them here, then the office of Peter clearly belongs to the very essence of the Church. The essential aspect of the Church of Christ is her task to proclaim the gospel of Christ in the world and to make this message "sacramentally" present in that proclamation. The essence of the Church consists in her carrying out her kerygmatic task. This kerygma is the Church's "deposit of faith", that is, the gift that has been entrusted to her and the task that she has been given. If it is to be at all meaningful, the pastoral service of the office of Peter is above all a pastoral service in the sphere of the proclamatory expression of the truth.

II. The Truth of Christ in Dialogue, Catholicity and Continuity

We can now try, on the basis of this definition of the concept of the office of Peter in the Church, to approach the subject from the Protestant point of view. In this, it hardly needs to be emphasized that this will consist not of a simple reflection of the Roman Catholic view, but rather of a Protestant interpretation of the Catholic understanding of the Petrine office. In connection with the problem, three points may be borne in mind.

In the first place, the essence of the truth of Christ and indeed the essence of any historical truth whatever is always to be found in dialogue. The truth of an historical claim or the truth of an historical event can never be a simple objective fact, something that is, in itself and quite apart from people, simply "as it is". Quite on the contrary, truth in cases such as this can only exist in dialogue between people, in discussion, argument, agreement and disagreement. A discussion can take place about the truth of faith or an aspect of faith and that truth only becomes tangible within the framework of the dialogue. We may go further and say that even the truth of faith that is being discussed is in itself dialogic, quite apart from its theological expression within the framework of the dialogue. It is in itself a dialogue simply because it is an event in which God addresses man and man responds to God.

There are, moreover, various ways in which a dialogue of this kind can develop. It is, for example, possible to approach the truth in dialogue by a fruitful exchange of divergent and convergent views and by being open to the truth in a critical and creative tension, while at the same time being fundamentally united in aim. On the other hand, however, it is equally possible to be quite closed to the truth of faith by clinging obstinately to one standpoint or by being intolerant and disunited in persistent divergence.

In the second place, the situation in which Christianity finds itself in the world of today is qualitatively different from that of previous periods. Mankind has grown much more closely together in the present century, achieving an almost world-wide unity, and this has resulted in a fundamental change in the position and the task of Christianity, of the Church of Jesus Christ in the widest sense of the word. Perhaps it would be more correct to say that Christians have become more intensely conscious of one aspect of the Church which has always been present in essence—the aspect of *visible catholicity*. This aspect has, as I have said, always been there, but in the past it remained in the background. Now that human societies and groups are no longer separate and communications are far more rapid, this aspect of visible catholicity in the Church has assumed a greater urgency. After all, the essential structures of the Church are not all equally developed at all periods in the Church's history. Now that mankind is almost completely one and undivided, the Church must appear to the world above all as visibly unanimous and united in the service of man, if she is to do justice to her task of proclaiming the gospel of Christ.

In the third place, the idea of a *continuity of faith*, which may be called "infallibility", is not entirely alien to the Protestant conception of the Church. The First Vatican Council, in defining infallibility, was referring primarily not to the pope, but to the Church as such. The Protestant too can agree with the idea of the infallibility of the Church as such, in the sense of the continuity of faith in the whole Church, in the sense, that is, of John 16. 13: "The Spirit of truth... will guide you (the community of the Church) into all truth". In this sense, infallibility therefore means, first and foremost, that the Church of Christ cannot lose her kerygmatic gift and task and that she cannot slip away from the truth of that kerygma entirely and for ever. The task of proclaiming the Christian message to mankind is not simply left to chance and pure fate.

I am not primarily discussing the concept of infallibility as a theme in this short article and for this reason it is quite legitimate for me to refer the reader to the relevant passage, pp. 161–172, in my commentary, written from the point of view of an Evangelical theologian, on the teaching of the First Vatican Council (*Die Lehre des I. Vatikanischen Konzils. Ein evangelischer Kommentar*, Basle, 1963). There, I went on, in a continued interpretation of the conciliar text, to give an outline of a possible concept of infallibility, in which I claimed that "the Church does not err in her function to proclaim and teach the gospel of Christ" (p. 164). The specific authority of an office representing this kind of infallibility cannot be expressed in "infallibly correct" statements which can be guaranteed to be completely free from error. This is because it is impossible to contain the divine truth which has been entrusted to the Church within a system of dogmatic statements (p. 168). The supreme teaching authority of the Church functions rather as a "pastoral care of theologians", a normative principle in the work of theological debate (p. 170). Within the context of ecumenical dialogue, this was offered to Catholic theologians as a way of understanding the Petrine office on the basis of the conciliar text as a supreme teaching office in the Church.

III. The Pastoral Service in the Sphere of the Kerygma

We have thus arrived at the point where we can define more

precisely the Protestant *placet iuxta modum* to a Petrine office in all the cases where it might occur. The Petrine office is a pastoral service in the sphere of the kerygma or of its theological expression. It acts as a norm in theological dialogue and as such safeguards the unanimity of the Christian proclamation of the gospel to mankind which has grown together in unity. As a pastoral office of arbitration, it has the effect of preventing theologians in dialogue with each other and with the world from being closed to the truth, either because of conformity and static attitudes or because of intolerance and extremism.

Let me give two examples of this as it occurs in dialogue between Protestants today. It is, for example, quite common for one group of theologians to accuse another group with an important view to present or a valid claim to make of proclaiming a "different" gospel. In the recent past too, when a rather extreme group of Protestant theologians asserted—not without good reasons and convincing arguments—that God was "dead", there was a distinct danger that all contact would be lost between them and the majority of theologians working in the more traditional fields of study. The pastoral service of arbitration clearly had an important function to fulfil in both cases. In all such cases, it can never have the effect of restricting the freedom of thought and discussion. On the contrary, it inevitably has a liberating influence and leads to a more authentic dialogue between the two sides.

A good example of this Petrine office of arbitration in the purely secular sphere is the office of the justice of the peace. The judgments that he passes have a certain authority, but they cannot be regarded as incontestable and it is perfectly possible to appeal against them. It is similar in the case of the judgments made by the Petrine office of arbitration—an appeal can be made against them, if necessary, to the highest court of all, the court of the individual conscience which is bound to God alone. This principle is also fully recognized in Roman Catholic moral theology, which teaches that every man is bound to follow his own conscience, even if it is in error. Despite this reservation, the office of Peter undoubtedly serves to maintain and if necessary to restore unanimity in the Church and it is there precisely for that purpose. This, of course, presupposes an attitude of brotherly love, of pastoral wisdom, of readiness to engage in open dialogue and of understanding of and respect for the views of others. If this attitude does not exist, even an office which has an authority which is incontestable and against which there is no appeal cannot effectively serve the cause of unity.

Finally, we must very briefly consider the theological value of our *placet iuxta modum*—"Can a Petrine office be meaningful in the Church today?" My answer to this question is, "Yes, it can, and particularly in the world not only of today, but also of tomorrow. I would go further and say that it can be meaningful above all in the future, for the time may well come when a universal Petrine office will be required for the task of ensuring a faithful interpretation of the gospel. On the other hand, however, the fact that the Church now has a Petrine office and claims that this was established historically by Jesus cannot be regarded as a valid criterion for that Church's being a Church.

Translated by David Smith

Hermann Häring

Can a Petrine Office be Meaningful in the Church?
5. *An Attempt at a Catholic Answer*

I. Fronts across the Confessions

IT IS clear, even from the many contributions to this issue of
Concilium, that the question as to whether a Petrine office can
be meaningful in the Church has been raised on several fronts
since the Second Vatican Council. It is true that various groups
of non-Catholic Christians have always recognized the papacy
under certain conditions, if not as the right form of Church
leadership, then certainly as one possible form. This is not a new
phenomenon. More recently, however, many Protestant theologians have been able, despite very serious reservations which they
cannot dismiss, to give their support to the idea of a Petrine office
as something which can positively help the one Church to understand herself and to make herself more convincingly present and
credible in the world of today. This is certainly a new phenomenon and it is very encouraging for Catholic theologians, who
live with the papacy, acknowledge it fully and are unable to avoid
being involved in the argument for and against it.

It would seem too that the confessional boundaries are no
longer marked off simply in terms of praise and criticism of the
papacy as an institution. Quite a large number of German Protestants have openly declared their sympathy for the strict exercise of office by the pope and bishops as practised in the Roman
Catholic Church, yet at the same time more and more Roman
Catholics are criticizing this practice in their own Church. Many
Protestants are calling insistently for stricter authority in teaching

and church leadership, while just as many Catholics are demanding radical reforms in the Church's understanding of the papacy and in the concrete form of the Petrine office as it has developed throughout the centuries. Is it not true to say that the fronts have changed completely? Are we not living at a time of great opportunity? In the past, the papacy was a sign of the division between Christians. Now, surely, it may possibly even become once more a sign of unity. The office of Peter has become an ecumenical theme again because Catholics measure it increasingly according to whether it furthers or hinders Church unity and unity between the churches. This criterion is applied equally to the office and to the person holding that office.

II. At the Service of a Scriptural and Missionary Church

This change has been made possible by the new idea of the Church that has emerged in Catholic circles. It is possible for the papacy to become an ecumenical theme because Catholic ecclesiology has become more ecumenical. The concrete results of this can be summarized under five main headings.

(a) There is general agreement among the various Christian confessions that the only legitimate basis for a valid ecclesiology is the *message to which Scripture testifies*. This implies, in the first place, that the only norm and unifying principle for every Christian message and therefore for every church is the person of Christ himself. Secondly, it is most important to take serious notice of the great number of models provided in Scripture for the Church. The Bible shows us many different church communities united with each other under the one Lord. Many divergent theologies are contained in the one canon of the New Testament. The early Church consisted of both Jews and Gentiles and the message was heard in many different languages. All these factors can help an ecumenical ecclesiology to work towards a communion of love and faith.

(b) There is general agreement among the various Christian confessions that their differing traditions and theologies and their different ways of thinking about and experiencing faith and expressing it in concrete models of the Church cannot simply be set aside. The extent to which these are legitimate in the Christian sense can, however, only be measured against the original testimony of Christ. Do they all still make it possible for the Christian faith to be accepted as valid in the world today or do they conceal the message under the veil of outdated tradition? This brings us to my third point.

(c) There is general agreement among the various Christian confessions that contemporary man has to be able to hear the Christian message beyond the traditions and to experience it as something that will set him free. All men have to be addressed by the Christian message because its character is essentially missionary. This is the prior understanding, on the basis of which Scripture and tradition have to be interpreted and proclaimed.

(d) There is general agreement today in many theological circles that the Church cannot be reduced either to the vague level of an invisible Church or to the coarse level of a *societas perfecta* precisely defined in legal terms. The Church is an *historical human community* and it is precisely as such that it is the eschatological proclamation of the word of Jesus, in whom God's word was definitively expressed. There can therefore be no anthropological or sociological law which cannot be applied to the Church. She has to make use of legal structures, organizations and divisions of labour with all the dangers and opportunities involved in them.

(e) It is not difficult to understand, then, that the early Church began, with the third generation of Christians, to build up institutional and doctrinal safeguards against her own disintegration. It is only subject to certain reservations and precisely defined criteria that this period can be designated as "early Catholicism". No Christian confession and none of the larger sects have been able to stay alive until today unless it has been an "early Catholic" community. Not even the conviction that the Church is a charismatically inspired eschatological community can do anything to lessen this idea. Any reference to the charismatic powers of Christian communities can only confirm the fact that these various structures are made specifically Christian only by the love which God sees in man, Jesus' brother. No structure can be Christian and legitimate if it stands in the way of man's love and service of his fellow men. The only legitimate structures are those which make the authentic preaching and service of the Church possible. The only truly Christian structures are those in which the members live lives of love and authentic service.

III. An Ecumenical Petrine Office

We should to some extent disregard the fact that there are signs of a Petrine office in parts of the synoptic tradition, because, as R. Pesch has already pointed out, we must be very cautious indeed in the conclusions that we draw from this. What should, however, give us real food for thought is that the non-Catholic churches have together set up a centre for communications in Geneva and, although it may not be permanent, it is none the less a sign that they have already, as it were, anticipated their own future. A. M. Greeley has spoken eloquently of the possibilities that are present in an ecumenical Petrine office that is without confessional frontiers. There are, however, at least three elements which are indispensable in any such ecumenical service.

(a) An ecumenical Petrine office must be embedded firmly in the life of the whole Church, that is, of the whole of Christianity which understands itself to be explicitly a "Church", and it must be nourished and sustained by the Church. It must therefore be capable of changing, just as the Church herself must be subject to constant change if she is to proclaim the message of Christ in a changing world. As C. Davis has correctly pointed out, the sacral character of the Church should not be confused with a lack of dynamism and authority should not be thought of as possessing a monopoly of truth. The most perverted form would undoubtedly be a Petrine office which was isolated from the rest of the Church and which had become quite inflexible.

(b) An ecumenical Petrine office would have to fit into the charismatic structure of the Church of Christ. Christ is the only Lord of the Church, the Spirit is the only giver of life and love is the only justification of authority in the Church. For these reasons, the power of an ecumenical Petrine office can only be a *service* carried out for the sake of the faith of the members of the Church. The Lord's words to Peter were, after all, "Strengthen your brethren" (Luke 22. 32), and the concept of "pastoral primacy" has been used in this context. A Petrine office of this kind can only be of assistance to Christianity and the message of Christ. It can give the churches a voice in which all men will recognize themselves. It can become the symbol of the commandment to love. It can make the word of Christ visibly present in the world. In the service that it performs for the member churches, it can safeguard their distinctive character and their freedom.

(c) An ecumenical Petrine office would therefore have to avoid the temptation to exercise power, to curtail the freedom of the member churches and to dominate the other offices in the churches. This does not mean that all outward representation has to be rejected. But the office of Peter must be able, for the sake of the brothers whom it has to serve, to dispense with all privileges, all imperial structures and all power.

Finally, there must be a fundamental readiness on the part of those carrying out this service to abandon the Petrine office as soon as the task that it is performing can be fulfilled more effectively and in a more Christian manner elsewhere. The disciples were warned not to claim for themselves the title of "master" (Matthew 23. 10). The Lord's promise to Peter (Matthew 16. 18) is contrasted in Scripture with his anger (Matthew 16. 23) that Peter was no longer thinking from God's point of view (see also Luke 22. 32 and 22. 34; John 21. 15 and 21. 20 ff.).

IV. A ROMAN PETRINE OFFICE?

All theoretical discussions of the Petrine office have the papacy in mind, either openly or in the background. For this reason, it is important to ask whether the papacy could in fact take over this ecumenical Petrine office and carry it out as a true service.

Neither a primacy in jurisdictional matters nor the claim to infallibility has so far succeeded in establishing unity among the churches—this is a fact to which no one should close his eyes. The other contributions to this number of *Concilium* show clearly, moreover, how little justification Rome can find, from the historical and the exegetical points of view, for its claims.

None the less, on the basis of its history, its reputation and its position in the Christian world, it is an office which has important claims to exercise a pastoral primacy. No comparable office has in fact ever arisen within the framework of Christianity and

there is no other institution of such influence and potential catholicity—John XXIII proved how convincing and authoritative a
really charismatic man could be in this position. What is more,
the change that has taken place in this Petrine office has resulted
in a dynamic movement in the Catholic and non-Catholic
churches in recent years. It would be unrealistic and unhistorical
to overlook the possibilities offered by this office if it were really
placed at the service of Christianity.

If this were to be done, the papacy would inevitably change.
In what direction should it move? In order to be in accordance
with the Eastern churches, the patriarchal structure would have
to be emphasized once again, but in the Orthodox Church, as in
the Church of England, the basis of this structure is the sacramental episcopal office, so that the part played by the pope would
be that of *primus inter pares*. In this, a balance would have to be
(and indeed could be) found in the question as to whether the
local bishop of Rome should *de iure* have (because he has *de facto*)
an honorary primacy, as he would have in the Eastern Church, or
whether the bishop of the whole Church should *de facto* (and
therefore *de iure*) reside in Rome. Clearly, the historical development is of fundamental importance in the case of both views.

It is only in this perspective that the basic meaning of the
Petrine office can be made intelligible to Protestant theologians.
The papacy could in this way serve the Christian community in
various capacities. The pope could, for example, in the first place
act as a "justice of the peace" and as the spokesman for the whole
community. He could guarantee authentic balance in the sense
outlined above and freedom within the churches. The Petrine
office could function as a communications centre and thus be a
safeguard against the tendency on the part of individual churches
to sink to the level of provincial self-satisfaction or to become
mere sects.

If the papacy is to fulfil this task, it will have to sacrifice a great
deal of its present structure. Much of the existing building will
have to be demolished before the work of reconstruction can
begin.

In the first place, there can no longer be an exclusive insistence
on an infallibility which isolates the Church, is contrary to the
true nature of the Church and is based on too narrow a concept

of Christian truth. Secondly, the papacy will have to renounce its legally based and sacrally supported claim to the leadership of all baptized Christians. In the third place, the present narrow historical understanding of apostolic succession and the claim to a total charisma inherent in the Petrine office, which makes it difficult for the many expressions of charismatic gifts on the part of individual Christians to survive, will also have to be abandoned. Finally, the exclusive and authoritative structure of offices regulating discipline and order in the Church, legislation, teaching and preaching, the censure of theological views and the framework of the Vatican State with its claim to sovereignty and its diplomatic apparatus will also have to be pulled down.

The office of Peter depends more than any other office in the Church on its being carried out by a Christian who is a true believer, who truly serves his fellow men and who has a true power to convince them. Theoretical speculation and theological books and articles may prepare the way for, but will not cause a radical break-through. This will only come about as the result of a deep change in the concrete situation in which the Petrine office finds itself. Above all, this break-through will, if it comes about at all, be achieved by a "Peter" who really possesses a gift for religious leadership, an understanding of what constitutes a world Church and an insight into the basic needs of mankind today.

V. Can the Petrine Office be meaningful in the Church?

At the recent international theological conference in Brussels, a resolution (No. 19) was passed expressing the conviction that there have undoubtedly been various types of Church structures in the New Testament and throughout the whole history of the Church. The Petrine office is therefore not inalienable and it can assume many different forms. Whatever form it may take as an institution, however, there is always the grave danger that it may be exercised badly and presumptuously. For this reason, it is more likely than any other office of the Church to give rise to a division between Christians, to make the Christian message incredible or very difficult to accept, to lead to dissent among those who should be united in brotherly love and to cause scandal in the world as a whole.

Because these criticisms are made of the Roman institution of the papacy, the "Petrine office" is referred to here with some caution. The concept certainly indicates the origin and the normative value of this function and service which forms, in my opinion, an authentic and desirable part of the structure of the Church.

Christianity as a whole has certainly experienced more than enough of the advantages and disadvantages of the papacy, but this experience should not prevent us from hoping that the papacy will develop other forms of expression which will enable it to serve the Church again in the future. It will, of course, never be a perfectly organized office and the man who occupies it will, like Peter himself, always be torn between confession and denial of Christ. He will know that he is failing when he is not sustained by the Lord himself—and by the faith of the Church. He may perhaps, in that case, be able to say clearly what really binds together in the one Church the German professor of theology and the Coptic street trader, and, for example, a revivalist movement in Africa and a Christian community in India. If so, he will perhaps be able to bring about true unity of faith in the Church.

Translated by David Smith

PART II
BULLETIN

Paul de Vooght

The Results of
Recent Historical Research on
Conciliarism

THE crux of the Conciliarist controversy is to be found in the
decree issued by the Council of Constance on 6 April 1415, known
from its first three words as *Haec sancta synodus* (H.S.S.). The
essential portion is this:

> In the name of the holy and indivisible Trinity, Father, Son
> and Holy Spirit, Amen. This Sacred Synod of Constance, con-
> stituting a general council legitimately assembled in the Holy
> Spirit for the purpose of extirpating the present schism and in
> order to bring about the unity and reform of the Church of
> God, in its head and in its members, to the glory of Almighty
> God, orders, defines, ordains, decrees and declares the follow-
> ing in order more easily, more surely, more fully and more
> freely to achieve the unity and reform of the Church of God. It
> declares first that, assembled legitimately in the Holy Spirit,
> constituting a general council and representing the militant
> Catholic Church, it holds directly from Christ the authority
> which everyone is held to obey, whatever degree of dignity—
> even papal—he may hold, in all that concerns faith, the extir-
> pation of the present schism and the general reform of the
> Church of God already mentioned, in its head and in its mem-
> bers. It further declares that anyone, whatever condition, state
> or dignity—even papal—he may hold, who obstinately refuses
> to obey the precepts of this Sacred Synod, or of any other
> legitimately assembled general council, both in the above-men-
> tioned matters and in any other of their acts past or to come,

should he not recant, is to receive the appropriate penalty and be justly punished, even if it should be necessary to have recourse to the other resources of the law.[1]

This text has given rise to any number of controversies over the years. It has been invoked by the supporters of Conciliarism since the pontificate of Eugene IV (1431–47), and later by all forms of Gallicanism and by Febronianism. It has been contested by all the strains of thought that can be grouped, doubtless somewhat *grosso modo*, under the heading of Ultramontanism. For many theologians, it received the *coup de grâce* from the definition of the primacy and infallibility of the pope in 1870. But recent historical research has completely changed this conclusion.

The results of this can conveniently be logically grouped under two headings: the historical consequences as such, and their implications for theological development. The documentation on both is extensive, and it is possible, within the limits of this Bulletin, only to refer to the main currents and cite the major names. To follow the matter in greater detail, may I refer the reader to my book, *Les pouvoirs du concile et l'autorité du pape au concile de Constance*, in the collection *Unam Sanctam* published by du Cerf in Paris, No. 56 (*Les pouvoirs . . .*), and my article, "Les controverses récentes sur les pouvoirs du concile et l'autorité du pape au concile de Constance", in *Revue théologique de Louvain*, Vol. I (1970), pp. 45–75 ("Controverses . . .").

I. The Historical Consequences

The ground has been amply covered, from the strictly historical point of view, by two writers whose works are unanimously recognized, Brian Tierney[2] and H. Zimmerman.[3] Tierney has shown that there was, *from the twelfth century onwards*, a current among canonists favourable to the *limitation of papal powers*, either by the college of cardinals or by the ecumenical council. The contrary current found doughty champions among the great theologians of the thirteenth century, but then the

---

[1] *Conciliorum Oecumenicorum Decreta* (Basle, 1962), p. 385.
[2] B. Tierney, *Foundations of the Conciliar Theory* (Cambridge, 1955).
[3] H. Zimmerman, *Papstabzetsungen des Mittelalters* (Graz, 1968).

"conciliarist" movement regained strength and vigour in the four-teenth, reaching its zenith when the Council of Constance met to put an end to forty years of schism. Zimmerman, for his part, shows that limitation of papal power by a council was frequently practised in the Church before it became a matter for juridical dissertations—in the tenth century there were as many popes deposed as there were elected!

The combined result of their researches, even though they approach the question from different angles, is that the Council of Constance, in proclaiming the decree H.S.S., can no longer be seen, as people liked to think, as having taken an unheard-of initiative or having indulged in unseemly excesses stemming from hasty and unconsidered improvisations. The council issued a decree which, though by no means devoid of ambiguities, was well rooted in canonical tradition, and which, above all, was successful in putting an end to forty years of disastrous schism.

The (false) conviction that H.S.S. was aberrant and heretical had led theologians, particularly during the last hundred years, to produce a closely knit web of affirmations which, though per-fectly coherent one with another, have today been strictly nulli-fied by historical research.

To take the events preceding H.S.S. first: from the beginning of the schism, so it seemed, it had been clear that Urban VI (1378–89) was the legitimate pope. From this it would follow that his successors were too, and that Clement VII (1378–94), Benedict XIII (1394–1424), then, after the Council of Pisa in 1409, Alexander V (1409–1410) and John XXIII (1410–1415), were anti-popes. The third pope in succession to Urban VI, Gregory XIII (1406–1415), would then have been the legitimate pope at the opening of the Council of Constance. And he did not consent to abdicate, as he was invited to do by the council, except on condition that he was allowed to convoke the council.

This formality seems strange, as the council had already been convoked by John XXIII, who had for some months been *de facto* pope. But many theologians found it significant, because since Gregory XII was the legitimate pope, he legitimized the council by convoking it. By then abdicating, he gave the council full power to institute proceedings against the anti-popes John XXIII and Benedict XIII and to elect a new pope.

But recent historical investigations shows this version of events to be a fairy story on all counts. Seidlmayer[4] and Přerovski[5] have confirmed beyond doubt the conclusion already reached by Valois[6] at the beginning of this century that both Pisa and Constance gave up all hope of deciding who was the true pope and that today there is no hope of deciding the issue either. The Councils of Pisa and Constance were therefore ecumenical councils and John XXIII was a legitimate pope. The irrefutable proof of these two points has been added by Fink, in that this was the unanimous view at the time and that from the beginning of the Council of Pisa, Gregory XII and Benedict XIII were both regarded as schismatic popes.[7] Fink has also shown that the concession the council made to Gregory XII in allowing him to "convoke" it was a pure formality, designed to soften the impact of his forced abdication. In fact the council offered the same sop to Benedict XIII. There could surely be no more convincing evidence that the council had no intention of thereby recognizing the legitimacy of one or the other.

Equally serious errors concerning the preparation and promulgation of the decree H.S.S. have now been rectified. When it was taken for granted that H.S.S. was a false step, it was necessary to show it to be invalid at any price. So it was obstinately repeated that neither Cardinal Zabarella nor the other cardinals present approved the promulgation of the decree, and that, according to the teaching of d'Ailly himself, it was therefore without validity. Historical research has now shown that the text that Zabarella preferred was no different in any essential respect from the final text, that the cardinals present unanimously approved this final text, and that d'Ailly did not consider the presence of the cardinals absolutely necessary.[8]

So a whole pseudo-historical construction, built on the pillars

[4] M. Seidlmayer, *Die Anfänge des Grossen abendländischen Schismas* (Münster, 1940).

[5] O. Přerovski, *L'elezione di Urbana VI e l'insorgere dello scisma d'Occidente* (Rome, 1960).

[6] N. Valois, *La France et le Grand Schisme d'Occident*, Vol. IV (Paris, 1902), pp. 502 ff.

[7] K.-A. Fink, "Zur Beurteilung des Grosen abendländischen Schismas", in *Zeitschrift für Kirchengeschichte*, 73 (1962), pp. 335-43.

[8] *Les pouvoirs* ..., pp. 29 f.; "Controverses...", pp. 52-6.

of the unheard-of character of a council acting against a pope, Gregory XII's elevation of Constance to the status of an ecumenical council, and the invalidity of the fourth and fifth sessions in general and the worrying H.S.S. in particular, has come tumbling down like a house of cards. This points up an important truth: it is not the Council of Constance that is legitimate because (and to the extent that) Martin V, the pope it elected, approved it, but Martin V who is a legitimate pope because, without any papal approval, the Council of Constance legitimately appointed him. The question of whether or not Martin V gave his assent to the decree H.S.S. then becomes of secondary interest, since none of his actions as pope could have been legitimate except to the extent that the council was legitimate, before him and without him.

Nevertheless, a close study of Martin V's attitude to the council is not without interest. This study shows, basically, that even if he did not make any solemn juridical act of approbation, his whole pontificate is still marked by his absolute respect for the council, his unrestricted agreement with its decisions and his continued will to obey these. Fink's study of the archives of his pontificate has brought to light dozens of instances where Martin has marked his disagreement on documents submitted to him by noting, without further elaboration: *contra constitutiones et statuta concilii Constantiniensis.*[9] In his bulls, Martin always refers to the *Sacrum generale Concilium Constantiense*, without distinguishing between its acts before and after the convocation by Gregory XII, or those preceding and post-dating his own election. In the bull *Inter cunctas*, he requires recognition of the Council of Constance in the same degree as any other ecumenical council, and justifies his action against the Wycliffians and the Hussites by appealing to a time when the council had not received the approbation of any pope.[10]

Furthermore, in 1421 and the following years, when Spain still upheld Benedict XIII against him, he specifically invoked against the recalcitrant Spaniards, "salutary decisions for the reunification of the Church taken by the Council of Constance",

[9] K.-A. Fink, "Die konziliare Idee im späten Mittelalter", in *Vorträge und Forschungen*, Vol. 9 (Constance/Stuttgart, 1965), p. 130. Cf. *Les pouvoirs . . .*, pp. 70–72.

[10] *Ibid.*; "Controverses . . .", pp. 58–61.

and points out to them that none of these will ever be changed: *"sicut ei diximus, nihil per nos unquam extitit immutatum"*.[11] Anyone who examines Martin's overall *prise de position* impartially must conclude that it eloquently supports his spontaneous declaration during the last session of the council, when, exasperated by the Poles, who wanted him to approve a decision not yet discussed in general session, he declared: "I admit and will hold integrally everything that has been decided conciliarly by the present Holy General Council of Constance in matters of faith. I approve and ratify everything that has been done conciliarly in matters of faith, all that and nothing but that."[12] It is clearly vain to try to exclude the decree H.S.S. from this declaration, since Martin V himself included it in his struggle against the last supporters of Benedict XIII.

The only difficulty that might be held to stand in the way of such otherwise unanimous evidence is that in May 1418 Martin issued, in contradiction to the policy of his entire pontificate, a bull forbidding any appeal previously made to the pope to be referred to the council. But here, too, some commentators have taken their wishes for reality. What the sources describe is not in fact a bull, but a project or outline of an act which, according to all the available evidence, never saw the light of day. Furthermore, according to Gerson and Wordmitt (Procurator General of the Teutonic Order at Constance), whose testimonies agree on this point, it was not a question of a general prohibition of appeals to the council, but referred solely to the inadmissibility of a new demand from the Polish faction in their attempts to push their particular case.[13]

As for Eugene IV, let it suffice to recall here that his pronouncements throughout his pontificate show the greatest possible versatility in the successive positions he adopted and a similar degree of confusion in the arguments he deployed in support of them. He can equally well be invoked as having defended H.S.S. (even in its most extreme interpretation) as having rejected it.[14]

It is not an exaggeration to say that recent historical research

[11] *Les pouvoirs* . . . , pp. 69 f.; "Controverses . . .", pp. 61–2.
[12] *Les pouvoirs* . . . , pp. 73–5.
[13] *Les pouvoirs* . . . , pp. 74–6; "Controverses . . .", pp. 63–7.
[14] *Les pouvoirs* . . . , ch. 3; "Controverses . . .", pp. 67–8.

has brought the precise sequence of events in the promulgation of H.S.S. to light, as well as situating it in its true historical context. This has allowed theological investigation to develop on the basis of a correct reading of the famous decree. Yet even if various errors have been cut off at source and theological room for manoeuvre strictly reduced, this has not produced total agreement: there are still differences of opinion even among those who do not regard theology as an astute game of fitting old events and texts into preconceived frames of thought.

II. Theological Differences

Some commentators, with Hubert Jedin at their head, would see H.S.S. as purely an exceptional measure (*eine Notstandsmassnahme*), which leaves the basic structures of the Church untouched.[15] This view is open to objection on the grounds that it fails to take sufficient note of the wording of H.S.S. itself, which indicates that its aim went far beyond just the Council of Constance. Neither does it take account of the fact that the decree, even though not a dogmatic definition *in directo*, nevertheless touches on a truth of faith, by its nature unchangeable and by virtue of this fact exempt from manipulation by any sort of "measure".

Others would unhesitatingly accept the plain original meaning of the decree but, judging it to be unacceptable within the Roman Catholic doctrinal tradition, suggest that on principle it should be possible for us today to understand the decrees of the council better than the Fathers of that council themselves.[16] A well-constructed hermeneutic then leads to an interpretation of H.S.S. in such a sense that it is no longer in conflict with Vatican I. In favour of this argument one can certainly adduce the necessary imperfection of any doctrinal formulas, none of which exhausts the possibilities of its purpose, and all of which are capable of being improved or completed. Or again there is the analogy of faith, a rule, still admitted, which allows formulas proceeding

[15] H. Jedin, *Bischhöflicher Konzil oder Kirchenparlament?* (Basle/Stuttgart), p. 11.
[16] H. Reidlinger, "Hermeneutische Überlegungen zu den Konstanzer Dekreten", in *Das Konzil von Konstanz* (Freiburg-im-Br., 1964), p. 225.

from different times and circumstances to be clarified in the light of one another. I do not believe, however, that a "better understanding" can go so far as to change the obvious meaning of a text. We are undoubtedly sometimes in a better position to grasp the significance and implications of a text than its original author, but we still cannot make him say something different from what he actually said.

In any case, these mental gymnastics are really not needed. Unless one interprets both H.S.S. and *Pastor aeternus* in ways that twist their meaning there is no need to see an opposition between Constance and Vatican I. The decree of Constance does not make the conciliar assembly the supreme organ of Church government, as the Council of Basle later tried to do. It does not demand obedience from the pope except in matters where he is in any case not free to act according to his own will. The pope cannot deny the Christian faith, nor can he create schism in the Church. He must govern the Church as best he can in such a way as to keep it faithful to the demands of the Gospel. This is what H.S.S. demands of the pope, and nothing more. It leaves him with the *plenitudo potestatis* at the head of the Church, but it also allows the council to impose its will and save the Church in such a situation as obtained in 1415, when a pope defaults gravely in matters of faith, unity and the pastoral virtues. But the pope remains the supreme head of the Church on earth after H.S.S., just as much as before it.

In the same way, Vatican I's Constitution *Pastor aeternus* is not designed to make the pope a sort of tyrannical despot, master of truth and error, free to act and make definitions at his whim. It is true that it gives the pope the right to make the final decision, without subsequent approbation from a higher juridical body (*ex sese*), but it leaves no room for doubt that *before* the decision is taken, and *for* it to be valid, the pope must remain within the bounds of good sense, of the truth ("For we have no power against the truth"—2 Cor. 13. 8), of the faith, of fidelity to the Gospel and the Christian tradition, and of unity with the Church, whose infallibility antedates his.[17] As the head is the chief

[17] On this subject, see a most enlightening article by G. Dejaifve, "Ex sese, non autem ex consensu Ecclesiae", in *Salesianum*, 24 (1962), pp. 283–297.

member of the body, but is nothing when cut off from the other members, so the pope, both before and after *Pastor aeternus*, is head of the Church, but nothing if he cuts himself off from it.[18]

The relationship between pope and council is too often presented as though it were a matter of deciding which holds the highest rank in the Church. In these terms, the Church comes, unconsciously, to be thought of as though it were an industrial corporation or an army, instead of as a mystical body from which no one can cut himself off without incurring spiritual death. In this body there are different members, each exercising its proper function, but none, not even pope or council, can create truth. All its members are servants of the Gospel, and all contribute their efforts to live and understand the Gospel; while it is the pope's function to make the final decision (*ex sese*) in the light of his attention to the voice of the Church and the Spirit, and so to be in one sense above the Church and the council, it is the council's function, at least when it is unanimous, to be the expression of the faith of the Church from which the pope cannot cut himself off, and so to be, in another sense, above the pope. But these concepts of "above" and "below" are not really suitable, reflecting as they do just those relationships of power, authority and command that the Lord wished to banish from the relationships between his disciples—"Whichever one among you wishes to be great must become your servant and whichever one among you wishes to be first must become your slave" (Matt. 20. 26).

For this reason, and also because the texts of Constance and Vatican I do not permit such a reading, it would be incorrect to assert that we must choose between a Church structured according to the Council of Constance and a completely different one based on Vatican I.[19] According to this view, the first would be collegial in form, and *ipso facto* democratic (and good), the

[18] In order to achieve this, the wide exercise of collegiality may well seem necessary, but it was not H.S.S. that invented the idea of collegial government in the Church.
[19] This is the basic objection that can be made to the conclusions drawn by M. Oakley in his otherwise excellent, highly serious and intellectually honest book *Council over Pope?* (New York and London, 1969), V, pp. 132 ff.

second an absolute monarchy (bad). These over-facile and fal-
lacious analogies with the secular political order confuse papal
primacy, a truth of faith, with an autocratic exercise of that
primacy, which would actually be no primacy, but a regrettable
deviation from it. But it would be just as possible for a college
or an assembly to fall into tyranny as for an individual to do so.
This is not really of direct relevance to H.S.S. and *Pastor aeternus*,
two equally valid documents each illustrating a different aspect
of papal authority. The particular lesson they teach is that just
because the papal office is singularly elevated in the earthly
Church, it is that much more subject to the demands of faith,
unity and an exemplary pastoral life.[20]

[20] The ecumenical character of H.S.S. was brought out for the first time
in modern Catholic theology by H. Küng in his *Structures of the Church*
(London and New York, 1964). The arguments he put forward there
have lost none of their validity.

Translated by Paul Burns

In Memoriam

PAUL EVDOKIMOV died suddenly on 17 September 1970, shortly after he had finished his piece for this number of *Concilium*. Those who, like me, had the privilege of knowing him personally, all recognized a man whose ecumenical zeal shone with a rare light. He spoke in the serene and convinced tones of the true believer, and his writings show us his deep understanding of the Christian mysteries. A theologian of Beauty, he was convinced that every painted, written and, above all, *lived* image of the Triune God forcefully transmits the invitation: "Be you one, as the Father and I are one". His last book, *L'art de l'icone, théologie de la Beauté* (Desclée de Brouwer, 1970), gives us his message: let yourself be drawn to the harmony of God, have the courage to rejoice in it and use this same courage to overcome all our divisions.

His sudden death deprives us of a much-valued colleague, but his theological and theologal thought will continue to encourage us in our ministry of *sobornost*: to seek the one and many-faceted truth along the paths of loving intelligence. May his wife and children find here the witness to our union in prayer and our common hope in the resurrection.

ALEXANDRE GANOCZY, *for the Editorial Committee*